VICTOR SEBESTYEN
THE RUSSIAN
REVOLUTION

'There will be revolution in Russia, and starting with unlimited liberty it will conclude with unlimited despotism.'

Fyodor Dostoyevsky, *The Devils* (1872)

VICTOR SEBESTYEN

THE RUSSIAN REVOLUTION

HEAD
of ZEUS

An Apollo Book

First published in the UK in 2023 by Head of Zeus Ltd,
part of Bloomsbury Publishing Plc

9 7 5 3 1 2 4 6 8

A catalogue record for this book is available from the British Library.

ISBN (UK HB): 978 1 80024 471 9
ISBN (E): 978 1 80024 470 2

Designed and typeset by Matthew Wilson
Colour separation by Dawkins Colour
Maps by Jeff Edwards

Printed & Bound in Scotland by Bell & Bain Ltd, Glasgow

FSC
www.fsc.org

MIX
Paper | Supporting
responsible forestry
FSC® C007785

Head of Zeus Ltd
First Floor East
5–8 Hardwick Street
London EC1R 4RG, UK
www.headofzeus.com

CONTENTS

The Russian Empire, 1878–1917

Map labels:

NORTH SEA
London
NORWAY (independent 1905)
SWEDEN
Stockholm
GRAND DUCHY OF FINLAND
Tammerfors
Helsingfors
FRANCE
GERMAN EMPIRE
Berlin
Potsdam
BALTIC SEA
Riga
St Petersburg (Name changed 1914 to 'Petrograd')
Warsaw
Vilnius
Minsk
Moscow
Vienna
Krakow
HABSBURG EMPIRE
Lemberg
Kiev
Kursk
Kharkov
Odessa
RUSSIA
Black Sea
Yalta
Sochi
Nalchik
Vladikavkaz
Batumi
Gori
Tiflis
Caspian Sea
Baku
Mediterranean Sea
OTTOMAN EMPIRE
EGYPT
ARABIA
Tehran
PERSIA

BARENTS SEA

R. Yenisei

• Kureika
Monastyrskoe •
Kostino •

• Solvychegodsk

• Perm

Narym •

S I B E R I A

• Krasnoyarsk
• Novaya
Uda

MPIRE

• Omsk

Aral Sea

Western border of the Russian Empire before 1914

| 0 | | 500 | | 1000 miles |

| 0 | 500 | 1000 | 1500 kms |

Gori   St Petersburg

Gori   Moscow

INTRODUCTION

THE MEN AND WOMEN WHO MADE THE RUSSIAN REVOLUTION wanted to change the world – and they did. The epic scale of their ambition is the most important thing to remember about the events and the individuals in the drama of 1917. The intention at first may have been to overthrow a Tsar and a dynasty that had ruled Russia for three centuries as an autocracy. But it went way beyond that. The aim of Communism, the faith espoused by the Bolsheviks who seized victory amid the Revolutionary moment, was no less than to perfect mankind and put an end to exploitation by one group of people – one class – by another. It was never simply an attempt at building a new economic and social system based on greater equality, but offered an entirely different way of looking at the world and history. The 'founders' Karl Marx and then Vladimir Lenin claimed their ideology was 'scientific'. But all true believers – and I met many truly brilliant examples over the years and in many parts of the world, whose consciences were sorely tested – always understood that 'faith' was the key. The appeal of Communism was religious, spiritual and the Party was the Church: 'I can see bright green strips of grass, clear blue sky and sunlight everywhere,' wrote Leon Trotsky, not long before he mounted the Bolshevik coup to begin the new regime of

Nikolai Lokhoff's *We Reign Over You*, an early socialist propaganda poster of the Capitalist Pyramid, painted in 1897, but banned by Tsarist censors.

the Soviets. 'Life is beautiful. Let future generations of people cleanse it of all evil, oppression and violence and enjoy it to the full."* It seems almost quaint to recall this kind of vision, knowing how soon it took for cynicism to eat into the soul of Communism.

The messianic scale of the Bolsheviks' ambition made the scale of their failure so vast and shocking. From day one the revolutionaries encountered the reluctance of many people – the majority, as it turned out – to be perfected in the way that Comrades Lenin and Trotsky had envisaged for them. This is the story of the early years of the Revolution – until around 1921 when the Bolsheviks had won the Russian Civil War, faced famine and disaster and reversed many of their extreme radical measures towards a new reformist course. I will show what the early Bolsheviks wanted to do – as well as how they coerced, bullied, bribed and terrorized their people in their attempt to achieve it. It will show too how they laid the groundwork for the outcomes that followed.

It is no exaggeration to argue that the Russian Revolution has had a more profound impact on the world since 1900 than any other recent event – and on historiography too. The history of most of the twentieth century has been a reaction to 'the spectre of Communism' made flesh by the Revolution in Petrograd in 1917. Fascism, the rise of Hitler, high Stalinism, the Second World War, the Cold War, America's policies of 'containment' to confront the Soviets' superpower status, the emergence of a new incarnation of Russian nationalism under Vladimir Putin – all are in one way or another the result of the Bolshevik Revolution.

By the mid-1970s nearly a third of the world's land mass was administered by Communist regimes – and the effects of the Soviet style 'experiment' continue to manifest themselves in profound fashion. The rise of China as an economic success story and world power dates

---

* Leon Trotsky, *My Life, An Attempt at an Autobiography* (Scribner, New York, 1930).

NORWAY

SWEDEN

FINLAND

GERMANY

AUSTRIA-HUNGARY

RUMANIA

TURKEY

ARCHANGEL

OLONETS

VOLOGDA

ESTLAND

PETROGRAD

NOVGOROD

PERM

KURLAND

LIVLAND

PSKOV

YAROSLAV

KOSTROMA

VYATKA

KOVNO

VITBSK

TVER

VLADIMIR

NIZHNY
NOVGOROD

KAZAN

UFA

VILNA

SMOLENSK

MOSCOW

RIAZAN

SIMBIRSK

GRODNO

MOGILEV

KALUGA

PENZA

ORENBURG

POLISH
PROVINCES

MINSK

TULA

SAMARA

CHERIGOV

OREL

TAMBOV

SARATOV

VOLHYNIA

KURSK

VORONEZH

KIEV

POLTAVA

KHARKOV

PODOLIA

EKATERINOSLAV

DON

ASTRAKHAN

BESSARABIA

KHERSON

TAURIDA

KUBAN

STAVROPOL

TEREK

TRANS-CAUCASIAN
PROVINCES

0   200   400 miles

0   200   400   600 kms

European Russia, 1917

from the unification of the country under the Communists, for good or ill. Mao Zedong's successors may have abandoned what most people think of as socialist policies in any way, but Lenin would recognize China's rigid one-party control under the Communist Party as familiar.

Many modern historians, whatever side they were on in the ideological/cultural divide of the Cold War and its aftermath, have used the Russian Revolution as their chief reference point. Some on the Left argued that Communism cannot be regarded as a failure because it was never properly applied in Russia or the Soviet empire in Eastern Europe and elsewhere. Many others – and not just historians of the Right – have described the seven decades of Communist rule between the Revolutions of 1917 and the demise of the Communist Party of the Soviet Union in the early 1990s as a tragedy for Russia and the world. Broadly, that is how I have tended to see it, as have most writers in the Western tradition until interest in Marxism and anti-capitalist economics began to revive in recent years. Many – perhaps most – historians from the developing world in Africa, Asia and South America have argued from a very different perspective. They saw how the Russian Revolution played a crucially important role in the process of decolonization; their sympathies lay in a different direction.

Was the Revolution a good idea badly implemented, as the socialists believed – or a terrible idea, rather more a nightmare than a dream, implemented with predictably disastrous results? This short introduction explores these issues.

Victor Sebestyen
January 2023

A NOTE ON DATES

The Julian (Old Style) calendar, used in Russia until February 1918, was thirteen days behind the Gregorian (New Style) calendar used in most of the rest of the world. Thus, according to the Gregorian calendar, the February Revolution of 1917 began on 8 March (Old Style, 23 February) and the October Revolution of 1917 on 7 November (Old Style, 25 October). This book uses the Old Style calendar for dates up until February 1918, and the New Style thereafter.

BARENTS SEA

KARA SEA

Olkson

Murmansk

RUSSIA

Yenisey

Pechora

Ob

Ob

Irtysh

Helsinki

Leningrad (1924)

Tallinh

Riga

Vilnius

Moscow

Gorky

Minsk

Warsaw

L'viv

Kiev

Kharkov

Volgograd

Irku

Rostov

Lake Balkhash

Constanta

Aral Sea

Sevastopol

Bishkek

Almaty

Black Sea

Tbilisi

Caspian Sea

Baku

Ashgabat

Mediterranean Sea

Tehran

Herat

Persian Gulf

Indus

Ganges

Red Sea

Arabian Sea

THE SOVIET UNION, 1920–36

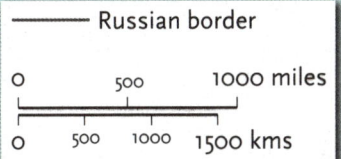

1

ANCIEN RÉGIME

1

ANCIEN RÉGIME

NOTHING DISPROVES MARXIST THEORY ABOUT HISTORY MORE categorically than the Russian Revolution. The classic interpretation from *The Communist Manifesto* and *Capital* insists that past and present are driven almost entirely by sweeping economic and social forces, not by the actions of individuals or even small groups of individuals. This story about the events of 1917 – the attempt to change the world through a fundamentalist form of socialism and its swift descent into totalitarian dictatorship – depended on the character and choices of a few key players.

Without the presence of Vladimir Ilyich Lenin in Petrograd in October 1917, there would have been no Bolshevik takeover – not then, and not in the way it happened. Even a man as vain and self-centred as Leon Trotsky, himself an inspirational figure in the Revolution and author of one of its most sparkling and brilliant histories, acknowledged the crucial importance of Lenin as leader. He said in the preface that there would have been no book to write if not for Lenin's role in 1917. The Soviet Union that Lenin built as the world's first Communist state remained a place in the creator's image until the end of its existence nearly seventy years after his death: intolerant, ruthless, ultra-secretive, ascetic.

Equally, there would have been no Russian Revolution if not for the weakness and sheer incompetence of the last Tsar, Nicholas II. The first, the original, the truest 'Communist joke' – a genre of dark humour that became famous in the Soviet world – was the comment from a Bolshevik commissar as early as 1919 suggesting that Tsar Nicholas should have been given the highest Soviet honour, the Order of the Red Banner, for his 'services to the Revolution'.

Historians have on the whole been kind to Nicholas II, mainly because of the gruesome manner of his and his family's death. But he was largely responsible for the destruction of his family, his dynasty and the Russian state as it had existed for 300 years under the Romanov autocracy, one of the most successful imperial families in history until he succeeded to the throne. 'Revisionist' biographers who suggested that he was a well-intentioned figure swept away by tides of history are too lenient on him. If at the start of his reign Nicholas II had made any efforts to establish a constitutional monarchy, modernize Russian institutions by introducing liberal reforms and allow political activity to flourish, he might have saved Russia from catastrophe in the twentieth century – and his life. He deserves his place in the dustbin of history. At a time when Russia needed wise and imaginative leadership, it was landed with a ruler totally unequipped for the role. The collapse of Russia's *ancien régime* came from the top. Under Nicholas, Russia was 'an autocracy without an autocrat' – an observation made frequently at the time.

Nicholas never questioned his rigid belief in the Romanovs' principles of monarchy. In January 1895, a few weeks after he succeeded to the throne, he told a gathering of provincial nobles that any hopes of liberalization politically were 'senseless dreams' and that he had sworn it as his duty 'to maintain [...] autocracy as firmly and unflinchingly as it was preserved by my unforgettable dead father'.

The Romanov Royal Family – Tsar, Tsarina, Tsarevich and four angelic-looking daughters, a photograph taken months before the outbreak of the First World War.

He wanted to be an autocrat but didn't look or sound like one, and he lacked the personality, the intelligence or the strength of will to be an effective one. He might have been a successful ceremonial monarch. His manners were impeccable, he spoke platitudes elegantly and he looked handsome in a uniform. But that is not how the Romanovs reigned. They clung to an archaic, semimystical idea of monarchy. He had a medieval belief in his divine right to rule, but no understanding of the nature of power.

He was not completely without brains. He was fluent in English, German and French and had decent Italian too. But it was said of him that 'he could speak several languages impeccably but had nothing intelligent or interesting to say in any of them'. Others who knew him were more generous. 'He was the best bred person I ever met,' said one of the less sycophantic courtiers. 'He had certain abilities, but they were limited by the tremendous parochialism of his education and outlook,' said another.

—★—

SOME REVISIONIST HISTORIANS – the excellent Richard Pipes, for example, in his groundbreaking *Russia Under the Old Regime* (1974) – have argued that in the twenty-five years or so before the start of the First World War Russia was on the road to becoming a modern European state. It is true that during that time Russia had boomed economically – up to a point. GDP growth from 1891 to 1910 was 8 per cent per annum, foreign investment was flooding into the country – around half of Russian securities, excluding mortgages, was held by investors from abroad. Alfred Nobel had turned the oilfields around Baku into the world's second largest producer of oil outside Texas. In some limited ways Russia was a dynamic place, though from

Nicholas II and Alexandra during the celebrations marking the 300th
anniversary of rule by the Romanov dynasty in Russia, 1913.

a very low bar compared with most of Western Europe and growth was slowing down after around 1905. But in many other ways Russia was entirely undeveloped as a modern society.

The numbers of urban factory workers quadrupled in twenty years, but was still very small compared to Britain, Germany, France or Austria–Hungary, the empires it was competing with to be one of Europe's 'Great Powers'. Industrial workers and miners – 'snatched from the plough and hurled straight into the factory furnace' in Trotsky's famous phrase – were banned from any collective trade union activity; until 1910 children of twelve were still working twelve-hour days in atrocious conditions. Russia's urban population quadrupled from 7 million to 28 million in the thirty-five years after 1870 but general standards of living and of health were shocking by Western standards. The death rate in St Petersburg was the highest of any capital city in Europe – far higher even than Constantinople, which was the next worst. There was a cholera epidemic in the city on average every three years from 1890 to 1912. In the winter of 1908–09, 30,000 people died from the disease. The Tsarist government did next to nothing to improve conditions of Russia's workers – an obvious fault, as the factories would be the crucible of revolution. Literacy had increased in the cities and towns. Russian society was becoming more urban, more industrial, more educated. Yet the Romanovs 'had remained fossilized in a Byzantine view of life', as Sergei Witte, one of Tsar Nicholas's prime ministers, put it.

More than 85 per cent of Russians, though, still worked and lived on the land. The vast population of peasants – the *muzhiks* – were still essentially without civil rights at all, though some advances in their legal status had been made since Tsar Alexander II's abolition of serfdom in 1861. Not, however, in their standard of living. Agriculture too was way behind most other European countries. Crop yields per hectare were less than half that in France or Germany. The small hand scythe was still used in most Russian farms at the start of the First World War – half a century or so after it was replaced in Western Europe. Emancipation was a raw deal for the peasants and caused two generations of resentment, perhaps more bitter than if serfdom had had never been abandoned at all. Peasants 'bought' their freedom – but it came at a high price and the majority ended up mortgaged to the hilt. 'Yesterday's serfs found that by becoming free they had become hopelessly in debt,' wrote Victor Serge, a one-time revolutionary who learned to loathe the Bolsheviks. 'They exchanged one form of slavery for another.' After emancipation the serfs ended up, on average, with 13 per cent *less* land than before to cultivate as their own. The peasants felt thoroughly cheated.

There was a sense of grievance across the empire: on the land, in the industrial workshops, among the 'nations' subsumed by force into a multinational empire where the ethnic Russians of 'Mother Russia' were a minority of the population (45 per cent) who held 100 per cent of the power. There were several Russias and their divisions ran deep: between the classes, the regions, the royal court and virtually everyone else; the educated and the illiterate; the land and the cities; between Western ideas and traditional Russia. The Tsars did their best to divide and rule to ensure the fissures continued and widened. But it was predictable – and predicted by many – that at some point the divisions would result in revolution and civil war.

—★—

THE AUTOCRACY SAW the spread of any ideas to modernize Russia along the lines of Western Europe, as a direct challenge to the Romanovs' 300-year-old dynasty. The Crown created an entire organ of state to root out 'subversion' in all its forms. As Count Witte explained after he served three years as prime minister, 'the Russian empire [...] became a police state par excellence.'

Tsar Nicholas and his father Alexander III imagined that tightened repression, exile for the mildest of political opponents, the ban, until nearly the end of the Tsarist era of political activity of any kind, would make the monarchy safer. They could not have been more wrong. The early Romanovs – Peter the Great, Catherine II, the first two Alexanders, were absolute rulers but possessed finesse and could compromise. The last two Tsars lacked judgement or wisdom. They retreated into the past in the hope that it would save them from the future. At the turn of the twentieth century, their great hope was to take Russia back to the seventeenth. It should hardly be a surprise that they didn't know how. Between them they made a series of fatal mistakes. Among the worst was to exclude almost everyone in Russian society from politics of any kind. There was never a solid, moderate middle class with a stake in the country's future. The vast majority of educated Russians, the *intelligenty*, were denied any voice in the way the country was run. So even conservatives who believed in modest democratic reforms and were opposed to revolution, were labelled subversive and pushed to the extremes. There was nowhere else for them to go. The Tsars guaranteed the growth of a violent opposition, which they were then too weak and incompetent to destroy.

The government had made some strides in furthering education; but this caused an obvious problem in itself. Students, predictably, were at the forefront of the opposition to autocratic Tsarism and the regime was constantly in a state of generational conflict with Russian youth. As Alexander Kerensky, the leading figure in the Provisional Government between the two 1917 revolutions, said: 'We all of us became the enemies of the autocracy almost as soon as we entered the university and this seemed to happen naturally.'

Nearly 20,000 ministers, provincial governors, senior civil servants and top army officers were assassinated by revolutionary groups in the last twenty-five years of Tsarist rule. Much moderate opinion blamed the government rather than the 'terrorists'. Foreign observers noticed that the near daily murders created no outrage among even the majority of people who disagreed with the revolutionaries; they shrugged their shoulders and complained about the regime. After Vyacheslav von Plehve, a particularly loathed Interior Minister, was blown up by a bomb in St Petersburg in 1904, the Austrian ambassador to Russia, Count Alois Lexa von Aehrenthal – not exactly a liberal himself – wrote:

> The most striking thing [...] is the total indifference of an event that constituted a heavy blow to the principles of the Government. One could hardly have expected sympathy for a minister who because of his authoritarian bent must have made many enemies. But a certain degree of human compassion or at least concern and anxiety about the immediate future would be natural. Not a trace of this is to be found [...] only totally indifferent people or people so cynical that they say no other outcome was to be expected. People say that further catastrophes [...] will be necessary in order to bring about a change of mind on the part of the highest authority.*

It was surprising how many of the terrorists were women – at a time when even the idea of votes for women in Western Europe or the US had barely yet become an issue of public debate. That there were so many young Russian women ready to kill and die for a political cause earned the radicals some sympathy among men in a highly patriarchal society. Sophia Perovskaya – 'a frighteningly single-minded' and

---

* Cited in Orlando Figes, *A People's Tragedy* (Jonathan Cape, London, 1996).

The Bolsheviks were highly effective in using posters for propaganda, often work produced by brilliant artists. Graphic designer Viktor Deni's *Capital* is a classic example.

fanatical member of Narodnaya Volya (The People's Will), one of the terrorist groups – was the lover of Andrei Zhelyabov, who led the assassination plot against Alexander II. She gave the signal to the bomb throwers who were waiting for the Tsar on the St Petersburg street where he was murdered. One of her co-conspirators described her as 'tiny, blonde, with pale blue eyes and pink and white cheeks like a china doll [...] a beauty'. She was hanged on 3 April 1881, aged twenty-seven, before a crowd of 80,000, in the last public execution in Russia. The hangman was drunk and there was no drop to the scaffold, just a wooden stool that the executioner managed in his stupor to kick away. Horrified witnesses said she took half an hour to die, in extreme agony.

Vera Figner, one of the first women in Russia to train as a doctor, led a revolutionary group which planned two unsuccessful murder plots against Tsar Alexander II, before her involvement in the successful attempt. She made a speech at her trial that was widely reported, though the authorities tried hard to ban any circulation of it. 'Peaceful methods have been forbidden me. We have no free press so it was impossible to think of propagating ideas through means of the printed word. If any organ of society had pointed out to me another course than violence I would have chosen it.'

Later, in exile in Switzerland, an equally passionate opponent of Lenin and Bolshevik tyranny, she recalled her life as a terrorist when 'the cult of the bomb and the gun, of murder and the scaffold, took on a magnetic charm'.*

---

* Vera Figner, *Memoirs of a Revolutionist* (University of Illinois Press, Champaign, Illinois, 1991).

Russian peasants *c*.1910. Russia's first revolutionary movement, the
Narodniks, believed that revolution would come from the peasantry.

REU

2

OLUTIONARIES

2

REVOLUTIONARIES

THERE HAD BEEN A TRADITION OF REVOLUTIONARY OPPOSITION to the Tsars throughout the nineteenth century, from the Decembrists' uprising onwards. The Decembrists were a group of aristocratic army officers who in December 1825, following the death of Alexander I – at dinner 'between the claret and the champagne' as Alexander Pushkin famously wrote – plotted to prevent Nicholas I succeeding to the throne. Most of them had fought in the Russian army that reached Paris a decade earlier and helped to defeat Napoleon. Having seen Western Europe, their declared aim was to build a constitutional monarchy and they dreamed of 'igniting a spark that will become a flame of liberty'. The rebels attracted an army of 3,000 to their cause and nearly succeeded. But they were crushed the following year. Five of the conspirators were executed and dozens were sentenced to exile in Siberia, including members of some of the most famous noble families in Russia which were traditionally loyal to the throne, like the Trubetskoys and Volkonskys. The Tsar's Act of Indictment against the Decembrists charged them with displaying 'the insane lust for change'.

For the rest of the nineteenth century, until the overthrow of the Romanovs, Russian political history was a repeating cycle of modest reforms, followed by periods of reaction when the throne felt threatened. Up to the abdication of the last Tsar one of the principal articles in the Fundamental Laws stated, simply: 'His Majesty is an absolute monarch who is not obliged to answer for his actions to anyone in the world but has the power and the authority to govern his states and lands as a Christian sovereign, in accord with his desire and goodwill.' And the Tsars meant it. Tsar Nicholas's tutor Konstantin Pobedonostsev, Procurator of the Holy Synod and for decades one of Russia's most senior civil servants, told Alexander III soon after his father's assassination in 1881: 'Russia has been strong thanks to Autocracy, thanks to the limitless mutual trust and the close tie between the people and the Tsar [...] we suffer quite enough from talking-shops, which simply stoke up popular passions.' He said the country needed 'a god-like autocrat' to restrain the anarchic instincts of the Russian people – a sentiment with which Lenin, Stalin and Vladimir Putin would wholeheartedly agree.

The structure of the police state was established under Nicholas I in the 1820s. He built an entire organ of government – The Third Section of the Administrative Department – to combat subversion. Essentially it was a secret service of the monarch, whose interests were seen as different from those of his subjects. Laws protecting property or the lives of other Russians were handled by a separate policing system. The Third Section – which in the 1880s was renamed the Okhrana (the Guard) – had draconian powers to detain people without trial and send them to 'administrative exile' in Siberia and the Arctic wastes on any hint of 'political crimes'. The Okhrana became the model for the Cheka, the NKVD and the KGB in the Russia of the future, or the FSB of the post-Soviet era. It invaded the lives of ordinary people. There were thousands of bureaucrats in back offices throughout the empire opening people's mail. The public needed a special licence from the political police for a vast range of innocuous activities – from organizing a party in a public place, to opening a shop, operating any form of public transport, to reading Darwin.

Tsarist Russia imposed the most rigid form of censorship in Europe, which obliged all printed matter to be cleared by a censor before it was published. With direct political activity excluded and reading political matter by and large banned, 'almost all literature became a criticism of Russian life, a social commentary, one way or another,' as Alexander Herzen, for forty years an exile, explained. Writers found ways to get round the censors, not always a difficult thing; on the whole, throughout history, good authors have been infinitely cleverer than censors. A highly developed form of *samizdat* publishing and of distributing illegal works, existed in Russia decades before the Soviet Revolution. Throughout the nineteenth century, censorship, police surveillance and prison sentences, were relaxed, tightened, relaxed again and became harsher once more depending on the political climate and the sensibilities of the monarch. But over the years thousands of people were jailed or sent to Siberia simply for reading 'illegal' books by writers such as such as Rousseau or Voltaire. This was no longer happening in the other continental European empires.

After liberating the serfs, Alexander II introduced a few other modest reforms; he permitted some jury trials, allowed an element of local government – the *zemstvos*, small-scale neighbourhood councils run by provincial gentry. He allowed travel into and out of Russia, which had been extremely limited. But following Alexander's assassination in 1881, his son retreated into absolutism. No substantial political freedoms were ever granted by the Tsars in the nineteenth century and they had no intention of conceding any.

The Russian monarchy showed no ability to adapt. The Tsars created the revolutionary movements, as one of the sharpest of the 'terrorists', Pyotr Tkachev, prophetically observed in the 1860s:

It is Russia's backwardness which is her great fortune, at least from the revolutionary point of view. In the West the social order is based on wide support of the middle class. In Russia this class [barely exists]. What holds things together in our country? Just the State – i.e., the police and the army. What is needed to make this state fall into fragments? Not much: two or three military defeats [...] some peasant uprisings [...] revolt in the capital.*

The Populists – Narodniks – were the first of the revolutionary groups to gain any influence. Initially they adopted entirely peaceful means. Their conviction was that revolution would come from the peasants. So from the 1860s bands of idealistic young men and women went to the country, tried to live in communes, attempted to open first aid centres and to educate illiterate peasants in a 'back to the people' movement that would lead them to a kind of pastoral socialism. Several of the type appear in Chekhov plays and stories. Most of them were from privileged backgrounds and were conscious of their wealth: 'Our awareness of the universal truths could only have been reached at the cost of the age-old suffering of the people. We are the people's debtors – and this debt weights down on our consciences,' as one them said.

Almost universally the Narodnik activists from groups like Land and Liberty (Zemlia y Volya) were shunned by the peasants they were trying to help who distrusted them because of their privilege, distrusted socialism and resented their paternalistic disruption of village life. In many cases they informed on the radicals to the police or threw them out of the neighbourhood – and in a few cases assaulted or killed them. 'Socialism bounced off the peasants like peas against a wall. They listened to our people, as they do to the village priest,

* Quoted in Vladimir Lenin, *What Is to Be Done?* (London, 1904).

Secret police mugshot of a young
Vladimir Ilyich Ulyanov, before he took
the revolutionary pseudonym Lenin.

respectfully but without the slightest effect on their thinking or their actions,' one of the leading Narodniki said years later.

The next generation of populists adopted more radical tactics. They resorted to violence to destabilize the state. They targeted Tsarist officials, provincial governors, police and army officers and their aim was to make Russia ungovernable. From the ruins a republic of agrarian socialists would seize power and transform Russia. The biggest and most dangerous of these groups was Narodnaya Volya (The People's Will), whose principal theorist and leader was the charismatic Sergei Nechayev, on whom Dostoyevsky based Pyotr Stepanovich Verkhovensky, the nihilistic central character in *The Possessed*.

After the murder of Tsar Alexander II, The People's Will was all but wiped out by the Okhrana. But small bands of (mainly) students, would form, disappear, reappear and adopt the same name, before disappearing again. One of these groups recruited as a member Alexander Ilyich Ulyanov, a twenty-one-year-old natural sciences student at St Petersburg University, who was hanged in May 1887 for taking part in a hopelessly botched attempt at murdering Alexander III. These ad hoc organizations formed later, at the turn of the century, into the Socialist Revolutionary Party, the largest radical Left organization in the country.

From the 1870s rival groups were launched, inspired by an import from the West: Marxism. They gave up on the idea of a revolution emerging from the peasantry, in a semi-feudal country like Russia. They believed that the revolution would be led by the industrial working class. A problem that exercised Marxist theorists – and caused endless disputes with the agrarian socialists – is that Russia was far behind Western Europe as an industrial producer and at the end of the nineteenth century had a tiny 'proletariat'. Alexander Ulyanov's younger brother by four years, Vladimir, would, under the name

Lenin, become the most famous of all the Russian Marxists, creator of the first state founded on Marxist principles. Many historians – most recently, Sean McMeekin in his *The Russian Revolution: A New History* (2017) – have argued that the reason Soviet-style Communism developed as it did is that Lenin tried to import a Western creed and philosophy to a backward country, as Russia was. Rather, the opposite is true. Lenin transformed a set of European ideas into a very Russian creation: Bolshevism. His version of Marxism, with its intolerance, rigidity, violence and cruelty, were forged from Lenin's experience as a nineteenth-century Russian. His Bolshevism had deep Russian roots and Lenin's ideas were a product of his time and place.

—★—

VLADIMIR ULYANOV – who adopted his underground pseudonym Lenin later in exile at the age of thirty – did not come from the proletariat for whom he proposed to make Russia's revolution. He was born in the small provincial town of Simbirsk (still called Ulyanovsk after its most famous inhabitant) on the Volga River, 650 miles south of Moscow, in 1870 into a family from the minor nobility. His father was chief schools inspector of a province, whose civil service rank gave him noble status. Nothing in Vladimir Ulyanov's childhood or early adolescence suggested that he would become one of history's great rebels. He grew up in a happy home, amid a loving family in solid, bourgeois comfort if not ostentatious wealth. He was taught by the example of his parents the values of diligence, thrift, hard work, and the importance of education. He showed no interest in politics of any kind until his brother was executed. It was a blow that devastated his close-knit family and radicalized an intelligent and passionate seventeen-year-old almost overnight. He, his mother and two sisters –

his father had died of a stroke when Lenin was sixteen – were snubbed from supposedly liberal middle-class society. This drove his virulent hatred of 'the bourgeois' for the rest of his life. Lenin was motivated by emotion as much as by ideology. He was often portrayed, on the Left and the Right, as an ice-cold calculating machine who operated on pitiless logic. But this was a misunderstanding. Rage spurred him as profoundly as any belief in Marxist theory.

After his brother's death, Lenin steeped himself in political works and the history of revolutionary movements in Russia. Though a brilliant gold star-winning student, he was barred from the best universities – Moscow or St Petersburg – as an extra punishment for his family. He obtained a place at Kazan University but was expelled after just two terms simply for being in the proximity of a political demonstration at which he took virtually no part. He was guilty by association with his brother. He lived at his mother Maria Alexandrovna's country estate near Samara and this is where he first read Marx. He claimed it 'was love at first sight, literally love', although it is clear the conversion wasn't in fact Damascene but took long thought and struggle, while he was translating *The Communist Manifesto* into Russian. At the same time he completed a law degree as an external student at St Petersburg University, cramming a four-year course into eighteen months; at the final exams he came top in the entire country.

He moved to the capital, tried and failed as a practising lawyer, but quickly became involved in illegal underground political activity – a notoriously effective debater against the 'Populist' Socialist Revolutionaries.

The Ulyanov style of argument was formed early and did not change significantly over the next two decades. He was nearly always domineering, abusive, combative, and often downright coarse and vicious. He battered opponents into submission with the deliberate use of violent language which, as Vladimir Voitinsky, a long-time comrade in the Bolshevik Party, wrote later, he acknowledged was 'calculated to evoke hatred, aversion, contempt [...] not to convince, not to correct the mistakes of the opponent, but to destroy him, to wipe him and his organization off the face of the earth.'

From his first days in the dissident salons of St Petersburg he worked out a method that marked him as different from other radical agitators – and, almost singlehandedly he changed the language on the far Left, which followed his aggressive pattern. For generations throughout the Communist world, harsh invective and abuse characterized political debate among so-called comrades – let alone between ideological opponents. The exchange of insults was justified on the grounds that this was how Lenin had done things. It was the Soviet way, inspired by the founder of the state, who created so much of the USSR's language, its lifestyle and political 'culture'. His successors, even after the Stalin era, adopted this method of derision and abuse. It was one of the principal lessons of Leninism: 'The harshness of polemics became settled Bolshevik practice,' as one of his chief critics put it, 'and the translation of words into corresponding action, physical violence to complement verbal brutality, was no more than a logical end to the process.' If you label opponents as 'vermin' and 'scum' it is a simple, straightforward step to treat them as such.[*]

It was a manner of argument peculiarly suited to Lenin's personality. He was never a collegial figure, but regarded himself as a man apart. He was one of the early members of the Russian Social Democratic Labour Party (RSDLP) but almost from the start

[*] Peter Struve, Collected Works (Michigan University Press, Ann Arbor, 1970).

assumed leadership of it. He was arrested for subversion in 1895 for writing articles supporting a strike in a St Petersburg textile factory. He was jailed for eighteen months followed by a term of three years 'administrative exile'. For social cachet a true Russian revolutionary needed prison time and exile in the Siberian wastes to be taken seriously, as a test of commitment to the cause.

Conditions under Tsarist exile were not as harsh as those faced later by dissidents in the Soviet gulag – Lenin married in exile and was allowed a gun to go hunting. But it was no holiday camp either. Over the years scores of thousands of people died in the work camps or froze to death in the northern wastes for no greater crime than reading or writing the wrong books. Some exiles had a relatively easy time. Others faced real hardship. On the whole, Jewish revolutionaries were sent to the most miserable places and suffered the worst neglect, part of the institutionalized antisemitism of the Tsarist regime; Yuli Martov, for instance, the Menshevik leader who was briefly the chief rival to Lenin as standard bearer of Russia's Marxists, was sent for three years to the freezing north of Turukhansk, where conditions were appalling. His health was destroyed and that was where he first showed the signs of the tuberculosis that would kill him before he was fifty.

— ★ —

LENIN'S GREAT CONTRIBUTION to the socialist cause was not as a thinker or in ideology. It was as an organizer and brilliant political tactician. The principal appeal he held for his followers was not due to the strength of his will or his manifest brainpower. His greatest skill in his early years was his ability to inspire optimism and hope. He told his followers that they could change the world in the here and now, if they followed a set of essentially simple-to-comprehend steps. He didn't offer salvation in the afterlife but a glimpse of heaven in the immediate future. Marxism is supposed to be a 'scientific' philosophy which can be 'proven' empirically. But anyone who was ever a true believer – deny it though they may – felt it emotionally, religiously, spiritually. Knowing the history of the Communist experiment in the latter part of the twentieth century, when zealots were replaced by careerists and cynicism ate into the soul of socialism, it is easy to forget the fervent idealism of some of the early Russian Marxists. In the 1900s nobody knew there would be a Mao Zedong, a Pol Pot or a Nicolae Ceaușescu. Lenin's appeal to mostly young people was almost always hopeful and optimistic. With the right organization and the right tactics even a few revolutionaries could bring down an empire the size of Russia's and an autocratic regime as powerful as the Tsar's – 'Some few thousand nobles have ruled Russia for centuries. Why not us?' Lenin asked.

The essence of Leninism is contained in his best-known work, a long pamphlet of around 50,000 words, *What is To Be Done?* Published in 1902, it made his name as the leader-in-waiting of revolutionary socialism in Russia and got him seriously noticed throughout Europe as a figure on the Left. It became the Bible of Lenin's Bolsheviks – the blueprint for how a small, extreme group would seize power and hold on to it. 'Give us an organization of revolutionaries and we will turn Russia upside down,' he declared. Much of it was specific to the conditions inside Russia and building a Party to defeat the Romanov autocracy. But much had far more general application – then and in the future. Mussolini learned from it; the Nazis studied it. The work was found on computers when US troops raided Al-Qaeda's caves in Afghanistan and ISIS camps in Iraq.

The revolution required a 'vanguard' of people 'who would first and foremost make revolutionary activity their profession [...] not

The Bolshevik photographer Viktor Bulla took a series of powerful portraits of Lenin soon after the October Revolution. From about 1920 images such as this hung in thousands of offices throughout the Soviet Union.

just for a few meetings, but 24 hours a day, having learned the arts of revolutionary conspiracy.' Such a party 'could not fail' he said, if led correctly. It was obvious whom he meant to be the leader.

One of the great thought crimes in the Soviet era was to be a 'deviationist' from the truths laid down by Marx and Engels. Millions of loyal Communists lost their lives in purges against 'deviation' under Stalin. The first major 'deviationist' was Lenin, who frequently turned Marxism on its head when it didn't suit his tactical purposes. 'For me theory is only a hypothesis, not the Holy Scripture. It is a tool in our daily work,' he said once, mystifying his audience. 'Lenin could veer, prevaricate, intrigue and sow confusion, seeking support from the devil if it was offered,' as Georgy Plekhanov, the most famous of all Russian Marxists before Lenin, noted.

Marx's *Capital* came out in Russia in 1872, just five years after it was first published in Hamburg, and fifteen years before it appeared in English. It was an instant success. Whether anyone read the whole of the huge book or not, let alone grasped its implications, its print run of 3,000 sold out in less than a year, while the German edition of 1,000 took five years to do so. Marx's ideas spread rapidly among the Russian intelligentsia. His emphasis that socialist revolution could be led only by the industrial working class seemed to explain why the Populist movement of the 1870s had failed. To the Russian intelligentsia it offered hope that backward Russia would one day join the 'advanced' Western capitalist societies. It would develop along the lines Marx claimed that Western Europe had from feudalism, through a bourgeois revolution to capitalism, the stages Marx predicted would 'inevitably' lead to socialism and then Communism.

Marxism had a particular appeal to Russian radicals entirely unsuspected by the author himself who had barely thought of Russia when he was writing it and hardly mentioned the country once in nearly 700 densely written pages. For many Russian intellectuals the idea that Marxism would bring Russia closer to the West was its main attraction. It would shine a 'path of reason, enlightenment and hope', according to Martov's intelligent sister, Lydia.

A significant difference between doctrinally orthodox Marxists and the 'deviationists' was whether a primarily agrarian country such as Russia, where 85 per cent of the population were peasants, was ripe for an imminent socialist revolution. This may seem an abstruse point now, but at the time it divided revolutionary Marxists as a crucial ideological issue. Lenin argued passionately that capitalism was advancing fast in Russia and the working class was growing, so it was ready for revolution. All that was needed was a push, by a Party organized efficiently, well led and centrally controlled. Others argued that Russia was not yet ready; the country had to wait for the various stages of development laid out by Marx. The issue was not merely an abstract argument about the finer points of ideology. Lenin didn't want to 'wait and see'. He believed in practical action now to make the revolution as soon as possible.

His self-belief and confidence were unshakeable. Splitting the Party and splitting again, remaining for periods in the political wilderness, would seem a hopeless route for a tiny group, with little popular support, to take. But in the long term – and Lenin was invariably looking at the bigger picture and the longer term – the tactic paid off. In his calculation, it did not matter so much how many supporters he had. The important thing was to have a group of people, a Party, loyal to him, of disciplined and dedicated people who would spread the true word. 'I don't want people with indeterminate views and shilly-shallyers. Better a small fish than a big beetle. Better two or three energetic and completely devoted men than a dozen dawdlers,' he told his wife Nadya Krupskaya. The biggest, irrevocable split came in 1902 in a Party Congress in London when the widest of the schisms emerged and the words Bolshevik and Menshevik first came into use as political labels. The main issues were arcane, minuscule. Lenin himself admitted that 'in substance the differences are unimportant'. They were mainly personal – Lenin saw Martov as a potential rival leader – and only a little about what kind of revolutionary Party the RSDLP would be. Lenin wanted a tightly organized, elite corps of dedicated and professional revolutionaries under a highly centralized leadership that imposed discipline on the membership. Martov had in mind a looser, more inclusive Party, less under the control of the leadership, where members had significantly more of a voice. The actual split was of a 'How many angels can dance on a pinhead?' type. There was a series of votes about Party organization and on one of them Lenin and his group won a majority, having lost all the others. With his characteristic mastery of tactics and presentation – spin in present-day language – he branded his followers '*bolchinstvo*', the majority and his opponents '*menchintsvo*', the minority. For the following decades, up to the Stalin era, the Russian Revolution was played out amid the rivalries of the Bolsheviks and Mensheviks and the stakes were of the highest – a matter of life and death.

Lenin's wife, Nadezhda Krupskaya, a revolutionary every
bit as fanatical and committed to the cause of socialism
as her husband. Often written off by biographers as a
household drudge, she was far more than that.

Nevsky Prospekt
*c.*1900:
St Petersburg's
main thoroughfare
in quieter times.

THE DRESS REHEARSAL

3

3

THE DRESS REHEARSAL

In 1904, a decade into his reign, Nicholas II made another of his disastrous mistakes, which added momentum to the revolutionary whirlwind that would topple him. He began a war with Japan for control of the South China Sea, in a bid to increase Russian power in the East. The Russians assumed they would score a swift victory that would give them a bigger toehold in Manchuria and the Korean Peninsula – after all it was, as the Tsar said, only 'yellow men, not entirely civilized' that they were taking on. But the Russian military was woefully ill-prepared and barely considered that Japan was modernizing fast and had military abilities to match its imperial ambitions. Russia suffered a humiliating defeat on land and almost its entire Pacific fleet. It had to sue for peace. Nicholas felt crushed. If he had possessed the imagination, he might have realized how perilous was his hold on the throne.

At home, support for the Crown was ebbing away among former loyalists, even in the aristocracy. The Tsar made enemies of the few business magnates that had driven the economic boom, Russian oligarchs of a bygone age. Nicholas and his courtiers thought it was beneath them to deal with people 'in trade' and the result was that most threw their support behind moderate liberals who urged Western-style reforms. Some went further. The vastly rich textile magnate Savva Morozov was the biggest contributor to the Bolsheviks: 'These days it is necessary to be friends with one's enemies,' he told one of Lenin's lieutenants. The wealthiest of them all, Aleksei Putilov, who employed 27,000 people at his vast engineering works on the outskirts of St Petersburg, and manufactured a large proportion of the weapons for the Russian army, said soon after the war broke out that 'Tsarism is lost, it is beyond hope.'

A series of strikes at the beginning of 1905 closed several St Petersburg factories, though they never looked like an insurrection. Some of the industrialists were prepared to keep the factories working by granting modest pay rises. Others, backed by the court, did not want to give in to 'industrial blackmail' and appeared to welcome a confrontation. The strike leader was a charismatic priest, Father Georgy Gapon, who believed that if the Tsar was told about the lives of ordinary Russian workers and was directly appealed to, he would intervene to force industrial employers to improve factory conditions and raise wages. It was hopelessly naïve, but he was persuasive and the workers' enthusiasm to follow him showed the faith the public appeared to have in the Tsar.

Gapon called on the strikers and their families to demonstrate on Sunday 9 January (Old Style; New Style, 22 January). He wrote a petition, full of humility and tragic pathos:

SIRE: We the workers and inhabitants of St Petersburg, of various estates, our wives, our children and our aged, helpless parents, come to THEE O Sire to seek justice and protection. We are impoverished; we are oppressed, overburdened with excessive toil, contemptuously treated [...] we are suffocating in despotism and lawlessness... we have no strength left and our endurance is at an end. We have reached that terrifying moment when death is better than prolongation of our unbearable suffering.

On the morning of the demonstration 'the sun shone brilliantly from a pale-blue sky upon the white expanse of the Neva and the snow-covered roofs and streets,' the writer Maxim Gorky, a committed socialist, recorded. The main body of the unarmed march was led by groups of women and children – 'dressed in their Sunday best'. Gapon was at the front of one of the columns, 'wearing a long white cassock, carrying a crucifix. Directly behind him there was a big picture of the Tsar.' When the procession reached the Narva Triumphal Arch they were charged by a troop of cavalry with sabres. Most of the marchers scattered. But some continued to march towards a line of infantry – and were mown down.

Some demonstrators made it close to the Winter Palace. The writer Maxim Gorky saw troops firing at them:

> bringing down little boys perched on the trees in a neighbouring garden [...] A sleigh drove swiftly up the Nevsky followed by half a dozen workmen running with bare hands and crossing themselves, some weeping. In the sleigh sat a youth holding in his arms a student, dead, his face one gaping wound. Three or four Cossacks came galloping up on horseback, pulled rein, looked at the sleigh, then rode on with a jeering laugh.

As the evening wore on the mood turned from shock to anger. One reporter, Harold Williams, writing in the London *Times*, saw:

> the faces around me and detected neither fear nor panic [...] but hostility and hatred. I saw these looks of hatred on every face,

young and old, men and women. The revolution was born. The popular ideal – myth or not – of a Good Tsar, which had sustained the regime for centuries, was suddenly destroyed.[*]

The army had repeatedly been used over several hundred years by the Tsars to quell domestic dissent – it was one of their principal roles and troops had been called out around 1,500 times against protesters between 1883 and 1903. But now, in the twentieth century, their use struck loyal supporters of the regime as a barbaric excess. Bloody Sunday, as it was called, was different from earlier atrocities in other ways. It occurred in Russia's capital where international journalists were on the scene, and the speed of communications meant the news was on the front pages around the world by the next day. Foreign governments were worried by the prospect of chaos in Russia. The American Ambassador, Robert McCormick, reported to Washington three days later: 'The events [...] weakened if [they] did not shatter, that unswerving loyalty and deep seated reverence which has characterized the subject of The Tsar of all the Russias [...] The Tsar will never be able to re-establish himself in his former unique position.'

The official figure from the government put the number dead at around 200 with 800 wounded, but the real figure was probably three times higher. In Geneva, a thousand miles from the action, Lenin was convinced that this was the beginning of the end of Tsarism – and that the end would not be too far away. Later, after 1917, he would call it the 'dress rehearsal' for his Revolution, as though it was all planned and scripted. Communist rewriting of history gave Lenin's RSDLP a leading role in the events. But in fact the Bolsheviks played almost no part in the initial strikes and unrest.

* Harold Williams, *The Times*, 10 January 1905.

The shooting of workers near the Winter Palace, Bloody Sunday, 1905, as depicted in a painting by Ivan Vladimirov (1909).

Nor did any of the other revolutionary groups. A mere handful of Party members were there at the demonstration on Bloody Sunday – and they were right at the back of the march, placed there almost as an afterthought.

—★—

THE MASSACRE did not end the protests. Sporadic fighting between workers and army units went on for five days in St Petersburg, and with more ferocity, in Moscow where scores of civilians were killed. Strikes continued for months, amid an atmosphere of government paralysis and political crisis unknown in Russia for a century. In cities throughout Russia workers elected representative committees/councils to direct strikes, raise money and organize protest. This was the first use of the word 'soviet' – which simply means 'council' in Russian – in the revolutionary context in which it became so well known. There was a mutiny in the Crimea fleet, celebrated in Sergei Eisenstein's famous film years later, *Battleship Potemkin* – and at least forty army mutinies among infantry regiments.

A wave of arrests followed Bloody Sunday. Gorky was picked up two days afterwards, charged with organizing a conspiratorial revolution, though all he had done was witness the massacre and write about it. Savva Morozov and other industrialists increased their subsidies to revolutionary groups.

Unrest spread from the factories to the land – worryingly for the court and the aristocracy. Scores of estates were burned down and their owners attacked. Many gentry landlords, or the intelligent ones, said the most significant thing about the 1905 'troubles' was that the attitudes of the peasants 'seem suddenly to have changed [...] instead of the previous courtesy, friendliness and humility, there was only hatred

Lev Bronstein – Trotsky – as a young man, pictured soon after his escape from Siberian exile in 1902. His other revolutionary nickname was 'Pen' because as a journalist he wrote so often and so fast.

in their faces and the manner of their greetings [...] underlined their rudeness.' Another big landlord in Tula Province, one of the most agriculturally rich in Russia, noted:

Externally everything appeared to be normal. But something essential, something irreparable had happened in the people. A general feeling of fear had undermined all trust. After a lifetime of security – nobody had bothered to lock their doors and windows in the evening – the nobles concerned themselves with weapons and personally made the rounds to test their security measures.[*]

In the autumn the Tsar bowed to pressure from liberal advisers in his civil service, led by Prime Minister Sergei Witte, and granted some of the reforms he had previously maintained he never would: political parties were legalized for the first time and a kind of parliament, the Duma, was established, though on a highly limited franchise. Censorship was relaxed and there was a significantly freer, though hardly an entirely free, press. The regime kept its hold on real power, but the October Manifesto did enough, for now, to satisfy the demands of moderate liberal opinion and bought the Tsar time to strengthen

[*] Figes, *A People's Tragedy*.

his ability to crush the extreme Leftist groups. He averted revolution this time but what he didn't do was learn any lessons or accept that the Romanovs could no longer rule in the old way. As Lenin put it: 'Tsarism was no longer able to suppress the revolution; the revolution is still unable to destroy Tsarism.'

— ★ —

WITHIN MONTHS IT became clear that the Tsar never intended to keep commitments which he said 'have been forced on me by duress'. He prorogued the first Duma soon after it began to sit and forced new elections on a gerrymandered franchise that guaranteed support for the Crown. Strikes and demonstrations continued – as did assassinations of officials by, mainly, socialist revolutionaries. There were around 2,500 of them in the two years after the October Manifesto. The regime used extreme measures to suppress unrest at a time when some civil servants were claiming that the government was introducing something akin to parliamentary order. More than 15,000 people were killed in those two years, at least 70,000 were arrested and 45,000 exiled to Siberia. 'Terror must be met by terror,' said Nicholas.

The Tsar fired Witte, blaming him for the continued unrest. He was replaced by Pyotr Stolypin, probably the cleverest PM he ever had. Stolypin was a highly intelligent conservative, an able administrator, who combined the first serious economic reforms in generations – he introduced radical plans to extend private ownership of land among peasants – with stern police measures against 'subversive troublemakers'. Thousands were hanged by 'Stolypin's necktie', as it became known, after 'field courts' held in the open air condemned them to death without any proper trial. At the end of 1906, eighty-two of Russia's eighty-seven provinces were under martial law. Uncounted numbers were taken away to exile by 'Stolypin's wagons'. Whole villages were razed to the ground – 'The Tsar went to war against his people,' as one highly placed civil servant put it. 'It's a total Bacchanal, of arrests, searches, raids,' said Stalin, who knew about such things.

Nationalist risings in the Baltic republics, the Caucasus and Ukraine were brutally put down, with many thousands killed. The idea that the Russian government was reforming along Western lines and introducing democratic principles into a constitutional monarchy is ridiculous.

—★—

YEARS BEFORE Mussolini's Blackshirts and Hitler's fascist thugs fought street battles with Jews and socialists after the First World War, Nicholas encouraged extremist nationalist groups to support him against democrats, liberals, Jews and the Left. He was an enthusiastic backer of the newly formed Union of the Russian People, which rallied to the support of 'Tsar, Faith and Fatherland'. He invited its leaders to his palace at Tsarskoe Selo, wore its insignia on his uniforms and subsidized its newspapers. By 1906 it had 300,000 members, nearly a hundred times more than Lenin's Bolsheviks. If at this stage Nicholas had any ideology, it was antisemitism, a common, a besetting sin, throughout the Russian empire. But the Tsar's hatred of Jews was visceral, imperial in its scope and reach. Many courtiers followed the Tsar's lead.

In 1905–06 more than 3,000 Jews were slaughtered in pogroms from the Baltic states to the Crimea. Most killings were perpetrated by extremists calling themselves the Black Hundreds, the armed wing of the Union of the Russian People. The authorities didn't organize them, but they did nothing to stop them. The worst was at Odessa

Pyotr Stolypin, Prime Minister after the 1905 Revolution – the cleverest of the Tsarist advisers. He was assassinated in 1911 and 'intelligent conservatism died with him'.

in the days immediately after the announcement of the October Manifesto. More than 800 Jews were killed, 5,000 injured and 100,000 were made homeless when Jewish homes were burned down. A few days later the Tsar sent a telegram to Alexander Dubrovin, the leader of the Black Hundreds. 'May you be my trusty support, serving for all and in everything as an example of lawfulness and a face of civic order.'

The Okhrana were ruthlessly efficient in suppressing the Revolutionary groups. Lenin had returned to Russia briefly in 1906 after the October Manifesto, but was forced underground again just a few weeks later and returned to exile in Western Europe where he would remain for the next decade. Trotsky had shone brightly for a few weeks as the leader for the St Petersburg Soviet in 1905 but was arrested and exiled to Siberia, though he swiftly managed to escape. Contact between the émigré revolutionaries in Paris, London, Geneva and the few remaining inside Russia was patchy. There were around 3,000 Bolshevik members in the whole of the country in 1912. The Socialist Revolutionaries (SRs) may have had more but not many more.

Stolypin's carrot and stick efforts to quieten the country were working, though the success of his so-called 'wager on the strong' in the countryside to establish a new class of property-owning peasantry was modest. Importantly, though, he had lost the Tsar's favour. But before he could be fired as premier, he was assassinated in Kyiv, probably with the Okhrana's connivance. Intelligent and rational conservatism died with him. The danger to the regime had faded for the time being, but hardly disappeared. Resentment ran deep, but so did fear and the realization that the police, the army and forces of repression were too strong, for now.

Sporadic strikes and violence routinely broke out and the possibility always existed that one spark could start a conflagration. In April 1912, 235 striking miners were killed by soldiers in the Lena goldfields in northeast Siberia; demonstrations erupted in Moscow and the capital. By the end of that year 2.6 million people in Russia were living under martial law and 63 million under 'enforced protection' which gave provincial governors appointed by the Crown the power to rule by executive decree. In June 1914 a wave of strikes began in St Petersburg and soldiers had to quell the protests. A revolutionary fervour was brewing in Russia. But the real threat to the Romanov dynasty would not come from Russia's working class or peasantry but from the throne itself.

THE WORLD AT WAR

4 AT WAR

4

THE WORLD AT WAR

MANY OF THE TSAR'S ADVISERS WARNED AGAINST INVOLVING Russia in a Europe-wide war that had seemed likely since the turn of the century. Count Witte told Nicholas that the country 'cannot afford to risk defeat because the army is the mainstay of the regime and may well be needed to preserve order at home'. He was thanked – and told to stop being so negative.

In February 1914 the Interior Minister Pyotr Durnovo, an extreme reactionary who as Police Director had ordered the destruction of entire villages and the murder of thousands of peasants after the 1905 Revolution, wrote a prescient memorandum to Nicholas warning that Russia and the monarchy were too weak to withstand a long war of attrition that would be likely in a conflict with Germany and Austria–Hungary. He predicted with remarkable accuracy what was likely to happen:

> The trouble will start with the blaming of the government for all disasters. In the legislative institutions a bitter campaign against the Government will begin, followed by revolutionary agitation throughout the country, with socialist slogans, capable of arousing and rallying the masses, beginning with the division of the land and succeeded by a division of all valuables and property. The defeated

The outbreak of the First World War prompted a wave of patriotic fervour in Russia,
– as it did in all the belligerent countries. This illustration was published in many
St Petersburg newspapers within days of the Tsar's declaration of war in 1914.

army, having lost its most dependable men, and carried away by
the tide of the primitive peasant desire for land, will find itself too
demoralized to serve as a bulwark of law and order. The legislative
institutions and the intellectual opposition parties, lacking real
authority in the eyes of the people, will be powerless to stem the
popular tide […] Russia will be flung into hopeless anarchy; the
issue of which cannot be foreseen.'

The Tsar's favourite mystic Grigori Rasputin, whom the Tsarina
trusted more than anyone as 'Our Friend, sent from God', warned
against war and predicted that if a conflict with Germany broke out 'it
will be the end for all of you'. Even he was ignored.

Historians who in general have little sympathy with Tsar Nicholas
have argued there was little he could have done to prevent war in

August 1914, that the rush towards a conflict by the Great Powers had a momentum of its own. But there is no evidence that he was in any way forced into it by his bureaucracy or by a bellicose opposition. He thought that a swift victory in a brief war would shore up his position and the record shows he was enthusiastic for a war that he was confident Russia would win with his chief allies, France and Britain. The Tsar 'leapt into the darkness without anyone pushing him [...] his much-vaunted sense of honour demanded it'.* Nicholas had a straightforward alternative, which was entirely feasible politically. He could have decided not to go to war, saved his life and his country from a century-long catastrophe.

—★—

In Russia the war began on a wave of patriotic fervour – as it did in all the belligerent countries. The Tsar was wildly cheered from the Winter Palace balcony when the declaration of war was made in St Petersburg – whose name had been changed overnight to Petrograd to make it sound less German. The pan-Slavic nationalists and jingoistic press had for long been clamouring for battle. They were convinced it would be 'over by Christmas' – with Russia in control of the Balkans and having achieved the long-cherished Romanov ambition of seizing Constantinople from the Turks.

The opening offensives went well for the Russians. They quickly seized swathes of Galicia from Austria–Hungary. But when they came up against the well-trained, professional German army sent to reinforce its Austrian ally, they were entirely outmatched and suffered defeat after defeat. They lost an entire army corps at the Masurian

* Robert Service, *A History of Twentieth Century Russia* (Macmillan, London, 1996).

Lakes, more than 120,000 men killed and wounded. The Battle of Tannenberg, just four weeks after the start of the war, was one of the worst ever defeats in Russian history; the entire Second Army was wiped out, with casualties of over 160,000. The winning general, Paul von Hindenburg said later that 'we had to remove the mounds of enemy corpses from before our trenches in order to get a clear field of fire against fresh assaulting Russian waves. Imagination may try to reconstruct the figure of their losses, but an accurate calculation will remain forever a vain thing.' The defeated general, Alexander Samsonov, went into the woods behind his command post and shot himself. Within three months the Russians had lost any real chance of waging an offensive war and were fighting to survive.

In the nineteenth century the Russian empire had vastly and speedily expanded eastwards and southwards in the Caucasus; it had performed well in the Balkan Wars (1912–13) – less so against the British and French in the Crimea (1853–6) and poorly against the Japanese in 1904–05. Its tactics had barely changed since the time of Napoleon; the army was entirely unprepared for a war of attrition.

Russian casualties in the early weeks of the First World War were staggering, far greater than anyone expected, and there were so few reserves that the army was soon forced to send untrained men from the second levy to the front. By the end of October 1914 Russia had lost 1.2 million men, killed, wounded or missing, a high proportion of them trained junior officers and professional NCOs. The commander of the 8th Army, Marshal Aleksei Brusilov, who would later become supreme army commander, said that the Battle of Przemyśl, fought that month in the Russian part of Poland, was the last in which he commanded

an army that had been properly taught and trained before the war [...] After hardly three months of war the greater part of our regular, professional officers and trained men had vanished, leaving only skeleton forces [...] From that period onwards, the professional character of our forces disappeared [...] many could not even load their rifles. Such people could not really be considered soldiers at all [...] the regular army vanished, replaced by an army of ignoramuses.

The reserves in the rear, he added, were the men who 'were the breeding ground for mass desertion, discontent and finally mutiny which created the Revolution'. These would become Lenin's Red Guards and willing accomplices.

The army ran out of equipment quicker than it ran out of soldiers. There were 6.5 million men under arms in October 1914, and only 4.6 million rifles issued. When war broke out the entire Russian army had just 679 motor cars (and two motorized ambulances). Equipment, including heavy artillery, senior officers and wounded soldiers were moved around from the railheads on peasant carts over muddy roads. The primitive state of communications was at the root of the military disaster. Along Russia's long Western Front there were just twenty-five telephones and a few Morse coding machines; telegraph communications constantly broke down. Commanders and their aides had to move around on horseback to find out what was happening on the front – rather as in the days described in *War and Peace*. Industry was not producing enough ammunition, including shells for heavy guns – partly because the Tsar and the court nobility objected to business people making too much money from war. The generals thought there would be enough for the short war they were assured of and made no contingencies for weapons manufacture after a few months of combat. Many battalions had no ammunition after just a few weeks of fighting. By mid-October 1914 some soldiers were

Anti-Romanov sentiment was fuelled by the scandals surrounding the royal
family's favourite, the 'Holy Man' Grigori Rasputin, who was often depicted
in opposition propaganda as the libidinous and corrupt 'mad monk'.

ordered to limit themselves to firing just ten rounds a day during battle. In many cases when German heavy artillery bombarded their trenches Russian gunners were forbidden to return fire. At the Battle of Przasnysz in February 1915 Russian troops charged the Germans practically with their bare hands – and when they were mown down unarmed troops in the rear would fill the gaps, with orders to take the weapons from the fallen men. 'They were flung into the firing line armed with a bayonet in one hand and a kind of bomb/grenade in the other.'*

Morale sank quickly, which the Bolsheviks used to their advantage. Brusilov said that after the professional soldiers had been wiped out in the first weeks of the conflict, most of his reserves could see little further than their village, or province and had no idea why the war was being fought. 'The new drafts arriving from the interior of Russia had not the slightest notion of what the war had to do with them,' he said. Russian soldiers preferred being taken prisoner to fighting. In the first year of the war four and a half times as many Russians were taken prisoner than were killed in action – 1.2 million to 270,000. In the British army that number was reversed with the dead outnumbering POWs by around five to one. As the war progressed Russian prisoners outnumbered the dead by sixteen to one.

—★—

ON THE HOME front, Russians 'danced the Last Tango on the rim of trenches filled with forgotten corpses', as Vasily Shulgin, an arch-conservative opposition deputy in the Duma put it. In Petrograd, the well-off were partying like there was no tomorrow – which, for

---

* Max Hastings, *Catastrophe: Europe Goes to War 1914* (William Collins, London, 2013).

many of them, there wouldn't be. This was at the tail end of the so-called 'Silver Age' in Russian culture, an extraordinary flowering of art, literature, music, design and science. Writers like Alexander Blok and Nikolai Gumilyov wrote their finest poetry, and Wassily Kandinsky, Marc Chagall and Kazimir Malevich were producing extraordinary paintings. The great bass singer Feodor Chaliapin was at the height of his powers; Serge Diaghilev's Ballet Russes amazed audiences throughout Europe. Sergei Rachmaninov, Igor Stravinsky and Sergei Prokofiev were in varying ways revolutionizing music. Russian scientists like the chemist Dmitri Mendeleev and the pioneer of modern psychological research, Ivan Pavlov, were winning Nobel prizes. But the reverse side of the coin was a 'senseless ennui', and a pervasive air of impending doom, described forcefully by the writer Dmitry Merezhkovsky. The epic scale of the bacchanal, the drinking and promiscuity, went beyond decadence. It was part hysteria, part statement of hopelessness. 'To what state have the Romanovs brought us? To the fifth act of a tragedy played in a brothel,' said Merezhkovsky, whose politics were of the Right. His wife, the poet Zinaida Gippius, wrote in her diary: 'Russia is a very large lunatic asylum. If you visit an asylum on an open day you may not realize you are in one. It looks normal enough but the inmates are all mad.'

Vodka had been banned since the start of the war, though wine and spirits were not, which didn't lead to harmony between the classes, or make much economic sense; the vodka sales tax brought in 20 per cent of the state's taxable income and its absence left a gigantic black hole in the budget. The poor resorted to homemade or black-market hooch to drown their sorrows; the rich binged on champagne.

Huge fortunes were gambled away overnight, while food shortages hit average families and inflation rocketed. The price of most foods, including the Russian staple, bread, rose around 500 per

Tsar Nicholas II inspects troops preparing for the Brusilov Offensive, summer 1916.

cent between summer 1914 and January 1917. Inflation in medicines was higher still. There had been long queues outside food shops since the autumn of 1915 and they were getting longer as the war went on. Camps with beds had been established outside some big bakeries and butchers. In January 1917 an average working woman in St Petersburg would work a ten-hour shift – and spend around forty hours a week queuing for food.

Shows of vulgar excess during wartime shocked foreigners and the middle classes at home. Sir Samuel Hoare, the British intelligence chief in Petrograd, grew to hate the Russian upper classes: 'Their wealth and the lavish use they made of it dazzled me after the austere conditions of wartime England.'

Morale in the army had sunk. Although the 'Brusilov offensive' of June–September 1916 in western Ukraine inflicted horrendous casualties on the Central Powers, it also took a grievous toll in Russian lives. By the end of 1916, as many as 5 million Russian soldiers had been killed, wounded or taken prisoner since the start of the war. They were deserting in droves. The President of the Duma, Mikhail Rodzianko, told friends that 'the symptoms of the army's disintegration could already be felt in the second year of the war […] Reinforcements from reserve battalions were arriving at the front with a quarter of the men having deserted.' The decay was not just among the conscripted lower ranks. 'Officers overstayed their leave, often by many weeks, and spent their time at the gambling halls and smart restaurants. Hotels thronged with officers who should be at the front. There is no disgrace in being a shirker or in finding a sinecure at the rear.'

The soldiers were increasingly weary of the war. This was the recruiting ground for the Bolsheviks and other radical groups. By tradition there had always been a large garrison of troops in Petrograd, principally in case they were needed to quell potential revolt. Senior generals were worried that there were now far too many soldiers crammed into the city – more than 250,000 of them. 'It is putting kindling wood next to a powder keg,' said one general, who noted that 4,000 men from the crack Preobrazhensky Regiment were shoehorned into barracks built for 1,200. 'If God does not spare Russia a revolution [...] it will be started by the army.'

Predictions of imminent revolution were on the lips of everyone in the intelligentsia, among Russia's upper class and the more acute foreigners. 'More and more every day the signs of trouble multiplied – and yet nothing was done to avoid the inevitable crisis,' Meriel Buchanan, the daughter of the British Ambassador to Russia confided in her diary. In January 1917 her father Sir George was given an audience with the Tsar – his last, as things turned out. He told the Tsar, 'if I may be permitted to say, your Majesty has but one safe course [...] to break down the barrier that exists between you and your people and to regain their confidence.' The Tsar replied coldly: 'Do you mean that *I* am to regain the confidence of the people or that they are to regain *my* confidence?'

The British Field Marshal Sir Henry Wilson, formerly chief of the Imperial General Staff, spent most of January and early February 1917 in Petrograd, Moscow and on the Eastern Front as head of an Allied Mission looking at what aid the other Entente Powers could lend to Russia. He reported back to London that 'opinion prevails [here] that the Tsar and Empress were a danger to the country and would very likely be assassinated'. His diary entry for 16 February reads: 'It seems as certain as anything can be that the Tsar and Empress are riding for a fall. Everyone – officers, merchants, ladies – talk openly of the absolute necessity of doing away with them.'

The Okhrana was aware of the public mood and repeatedly sent warnings to the highest levels of the government. A report to the

Minister of the Interior, Alexander Protopopov, in October 1916, stated in stark terms that it wasn't the revolutionary groups the regime should be worried about: 'It is the people.' The agent said that, 'Now anger is not directed against the government generally but against the Tsar.' The report told the Minister, if he didn't know it already, that the Tsarina Alexandra was invariably called 'the German woman' and that rumours about the relationship between her and Rasputin – 'which are extremely damaging to the government' – were growing more lurid and more scandalous by the day. It was also said the Tsarina was also having a lesbian affair with her lady-in-waiting Anna Vyrubova. It did not matter whether the stories were true – they certainly were not – but they were circulated everywhere, they were widely believed and they had a profound effect on the prestige of the monarchy.

Support for the Tsar was collapsing. Vladimir Nabokov, father of the novelist, and a leading figure in the opposition Constitutional Democratic Party (Kadets), a moderate reformer of traditional monarchist views, said that 'at this time, to be for the Tsar was to be against Russia'. On 5 January 1917 the Petrograd Okhrana was reporting to the Interior Ministry that there were plots to topple the Tsar by members of the Royal Family and senior centre-right figures in the Duma, who argued that 'we have to save the monarchy from the monarch'. The principal plotter was Alexander Guchkov, the vastly wealthy industrialist and influential powerbroker who founded the Octobrist Party, originally as a loyal supporter of Tsar Nicholas. But he had become exasperated by the ruler's incompetence and the court's inability to unite the country for the war effort. He had plotted a putsch, backed by the imperial army chiefs, to topple the Tsar and replace him with his brother Grand Duke Mikhail. The plan failed when Mikhail would have nothing to do with it. The only plot that did succeed was the assassination of Rasputin in December 1916 led by the fabulously rich and well-connected Prince Yusupov, once a favourite of the Tsar's. But that came too late to make much difference in saving the monarch or the monarchy.

In late January 1917 the Okhrana chief in Petrograd reported that:

The country is on a precipice beside which 1905 was child's play. The alarming mood grows stronger by the day. It penetrates through all levels of the population and there is the very strong threat of great turbulence, brought about [...] principally by economic factors, hunger and the unequal distribution of food and the monstrous price increases in articles of prime necessity. Until now this discontent has had an economic basis and has not been connected with a political movement. But it only needs something concrete and specific to take on a political expression. If bread becomes more scarce this will touch off the strongest kind of disorders [...] and endless street riots.

A separate report around the same time on the Petrograd army garrison warned the imperial chiefs of staff that 'if there is a revolution it would be supported by two thirds of [...] active soldiers'.

The intelligentsia realized things could not continue as they had. 'We know something is coming,' Zinaida Gippius recorded in her diary. 'But will it be "the revolution", or some monstrosity with an unknown name?'

THE
FEBRUARY
REVOLUTION

5

THE FEBRUARY REVOLUTION

The Revolution began almost exactly as the more acute of the Tsar's key advisers had warned and the Okhrana had predicted. The 1916–17 winter in Russia was the coldest of the century so far – and the weather was a significant and often underrated factor in what was about to happen. Temperatures in Petrograd throughout the latter part of January and most of February *averaged* minus 15° C; many days were colder. Transport links to the cities, including the railways, ground to a virtual standstill and little grain or other food supplies reached Petrograd or Moscow. The capital's Mayor reported on 19 February that in the previous week the capital received around 75,000 kg of flour compared to the usual 425,000 kg and city's bakers were allowed to use only 15,500 kg rather than the normal 135,000. Thousands of women – and it *was* mostly women – were queuing all night for bread. Then on 23 February the Arctic weather broke and the temperatures, as Gorky noted, were 'an almost balmy 5 degrees'. That is when a wave of strikes and demonstrations in Petrograd textile mills and industrial plants began – 130,000 or so people on the 23rd, International Women's Day, more than 180,000 the following day. By the afternoon of the first big street protests, people were no longer shouting 'We want

Bread' and 'We are hungry' but the demands had changed to 'Down with the Tsar', 'Give Us Peace' and 'Damn the German Woman'.

Mobs lynched police – they stoned the Chief of the Petrograd gendarmerie to death – and began to take over government buildings. They 'liberated' the Peter and Paul Fortress, and released the few prisoners inside, most of whom had been arrested only in the previous few days. Much of the city was in the hands of the protestors. The police could not contain the crowds, and the troops refused to fire on civilians. By the second day of unrest much of the city was in the hands of the protestors. That didn't deter Princess Catherine Radziwill on 25 February from holding the *soirée* that all Petrograd society had been talking about for weeks. In his diary, Maurice Paléologue, the French Ambassador to Russia, said that her brilliantly lit palace on Fontanka embankment and the opulence of the evening brought to mind the Paris of 1789.

The Tsar was no longer in the capital, or in his main residence at Tsarskoe Selo, about 17 miles south-east of Petrograd, but at his military headquarters at Mogilev, near the front. In another of his disastrous errors he had eighteen months earlier taken personal command of the army – against the advice of all his ministers and his Imperial General staff. It meant that when things went wrong he couldn't blame his field commanders but took responsibility for the conduct of the war himself. He had been told of the street demonstrations, but did not grasp how serious they were and believed the usual tried and tested methods against riot in the capital – sending in the troops – would be more than ample to suffice. Tsarina Alexandra, increasingly in charge of domestic matters when Nicholas was at the front, wrote complacently telling him:

This is a hooligan movement. Young people run and shout that there is no bread, simply to create excitement, along with workers who

Protesters in front of the Winter Palace, February 1917.

prevent others from working. If the weather were still very cold they would probably all stay home. But all this will pass and become calm.

He chose to ignore the more realistic warnings given by the Octobrist chairman of the Duma, Mikhail Rodzianko, in a telegram:

Situation serious. In the capital anarchy. Government paralysed. Transport of food and fuel completely disorganized. Public disaffection growing. On the streets chaotic shooting. It is essential at once to entrust a person enjoying country's confidence with the formation of a new government. There should be no delay. All delay is death.

Having heard nothing, a few hours later he sent another cable. 'Situation deteriorating. Imperative to take immediate steps for tomorrow will be too late. The last hour has struck, decisive as the fate of the Fatherland and dynasty.' The Tsar's only reaction was to glance at the telegram and turn to his chief aide Count Vladimir Fredericks and say, 'That fat fellow Rodzianko has again written to me all kinds of nonsense. I shan't even bother to answer.'

Nicholas ordered General Sergei Khabalov, Commander of the Petrograd Military District, to use any methods to disperse the crowds: 'I order you to use whatever force is necessary to stop tomorrow the disorders in the capital, which are unacceptable at this difficult time of war with Germany and Austria.' Khabalov said later that he was dismayed by the Tsar's instructions. He knew, if Nicholas didn't, that the troops would refuse to obey orders. The Revolution was sparked by bread riots but it succeeded because every regiment in the Petrograd guard – the smart regiments that for centuries had been fiercely loyal to the Romanovs – mutinied. It was troops from Russia's most famous and supposedly loyal army regiments, the Preobrazhensky, Volynsky, Pavlovsky and Litovsky, known as the Tsar's praetorians, who decided the fate of the Tsar.

On 26 February, a day and a half after the Tsar's order, the Petrograd Chief of Police described the scenes in the capital in his last report to the Interior Minister:

At six in the morning the telephone rang. The city prefect told me that an NCO in the Volynsky Regiment of the Guard named (Timofey) Kirpichnikov had just killed his superior officer [...] the assassin had disappeared and the attitude of the regiment was threatening [to other officers]. I now saw how far anarchy had spread and infected the barracks. A short while later the Prefect called again with more bad news. Brigadier General Dobrovsky, commander of a battalion of sappers in the Guards, had been killed by his men. The events moved fast. The Volynsky troops [...] chased almost all its officers out of the barracks. These mutineers joined the Preobrazhensky regiment, whose barracks were near their own. They succeeded in capturing the arsenal on the Liteiny Bridge. Soldiers were dashing about the streets armed with guns. A raging crowd invaded the Prison of Preliminary Confinement and opened the cells. Soon it was the same in all the city's prisons. The police stations were taken by the mob. Policemen who were not able to change into *mufti* were torn to pieces. Fires finished off the rest.

Mutinous troops and groups of workers to whom the soldiers had given arms roamed the streets attacking any authority figures they could find. It has often been said that the February Revolution was a generally peaceful uprising. This is a myth that has gained authority largely because it was genuinely popular, supported by the vast majority of people. But it was far from peaceful. Far more people were killed in February than would die in the Bolshevik coup in October – 1,433 in Petrograd, around 3,000 in Moscow, where armed gangs roamed the streets for several days. The October coup was almost bloodless by comparison.

—★—

AFTER ORDERING the troops to suppress the demonstrations, the Tsar prorogued the Duma. Again, his instinct when in trouble was to ban politics. But this time the Duma politicians refused to go quietly and when the following morning members as usual entered the Tauride Palace, built by Catherine the Great's favourite, Prince Potemkin, there was nobody to enforce the Tsar's will. With no government, anarchy on the streets, the army in open mutiny, mobs throughout the city shouting 'Death to the Tsar', they filled the power vacuum – or tried to – with a 'Temporary Committee of the State Duma'. First, the Duma established a Provisional Government led by an elderly liberal, Prince Georgy Lvov, who quickly formed a coalition of centre-right Constitutional Democrats (the Kadets), Octobrists and other liberals and moderate socialists, who would be in charge until elections to a Constituent Assembly which they promised for as soon as practicable.

Second, it had to decide what to do about the Tsar. They agreed unanimously that Nicholas had to go – but the Royalists wanted him to abdicate in favour of his teenage son, Alexei, and retain a constitutional monarchy. They were swung around against the Romanovs and the idea of monarchy by the liberals and Leftists – 'It is not only unacceptable, but also utopian, given the general hatred of the monarchy among the mass of the people,' argued the new Minister for Justice, Alexander Kerensky. They agreed they would force the Tsar to abdicate in favour of his brother Archduke Mikhail, who gave his word to them that the following day he would dissolve the Romanovs' claim to the throne.

If it was the army rank and file that took over control of the streets of Petrograd and Moscow, it was the top brass that forced the Tsar to abdicate, in particular his chief of staff, General Mikhail Alexeev, who withdrew the army's support for the Crown, supported by almost the entire general staff. The monarch was without significant support anywhere.

The dignity of his departure and his gentlemanly bearing should not mask how hopeless Nicholas II had been as a ruler, and in what a terrible state he was leaving his country. The Duma had despatched two right-wing politicians, Alexander Guchkov and Vasily Shulgin, to extract the abdication proclamation. The Tsar was returning to Petrograd from his military headquarters in the imperial railway carriage. They met him at a remote station near Pskov at 9.45 p.m. on 1 March. The Tsar 'was absolutely calm, almost impenetrable', Guchkov recalled. 'I even wondered whether we were dealing with a normal person. One might allow oneself some show of emotion on the occasion, but nothing of the sort.' A few words were drafted on a page. 'We hand over the succession to Our Beloved Brother the Grand Duke Michael Alexandrovich and bless him on his succession.' Fredericks placed the document on the royal writing desk. 'Then, bowing his head for a few moments, he dipped his pen and [...] for the last time appended his signature as Tsar of All the Russias to the writ of Abdication.' Fredericks said soon afterwards the extraordinary event was so matter of fact 'as if he were turning over command of a cavalry regiment'. True to his word, Archduke Michael renounced the throne after less than twelve hours as Tsar.

—★—

The hastily formed People's Militia, established to protect the gains made by the February Revolution, which forced the Tsar's abdication. This picture is among an extraordinary collection taken by the socialist photographer Yakov Steinberg.

THE LEFTIST GROUPS had played virtually no part in the Revolution, as Sergey Mtislavsky, a leading Socialist Revolutionary activist in Petrograd, acknowledged. 'We SRs were fast asleep, like the Foolish Virgins in the Gospel,' he admitted later. 'The truth of the matter is that outside of the small factions of the revolutionaries [...] slewing in our own juices, the socialist parties were completely bankrupt.' The Bolsheviks had reluctantly joined the street demonstrations, but had not led them. 'We didn't think this was going to be a revolution, so went along with the protests with a heavy heart, thinking they would be brutally suppressed by the Tsar,' said Vladimir Kayurov, one of the leaders of the Party underground in Russia.

The Revolution had been entirely spontaneous, an outpouring of anger – a classic example of a popular revolt against an incompetent and bankrupt regime. The Tsar's secret police had beaten the Bolsheviks and other revolutionary groups; but they had forgotten about the people. The British journalist Arthur Ransome began his 3 March despatch for the *Daily News*, 'Let there be no mistake [...] This was not an organized revolution. It will be impossible to make a statue in memory of its organizer, unless that statue represents a simple Russian peasant soldier.'

—★—

FOR THE FIRST few days it seemed as though 'a miracle has occurred and we may expect more miracles', as the poet Alexander Blok wrote to his mother. 'There is the extraordinary feeling that nothing is forbidden, that anything can happen.' After 300 years in absolute power the Romanov dynasty had collapsed in a matter of days, he said, 'like a train crash in the night, like a bridge crumbling beneath your feet, like a house falling down'. People on all rungs of society greeted the rising as the birth of a new era. Even a moderate conservative like Nabokov thought that 'something great and sacred had occurred, that the people had cast off their chains, that despotism had collapsed'. Together with Baron Nolde, Nabokov had drafted Grand Duke Mikhail's statement relinquishing the throne. At first he held high hopes for the Provisional Government and believed that reforms and a democracy for Russia was within reach.

The new government's first steps were hugely popular. It promised free and fair elections on the basis of universal suffrage for men and women; it introduced a free press and abolished censorship, legalized trade unions and introduced a maximum ten-hour day for factory workers; it promised widespread land reforms. For the first time in Russian history, Jews and all religions were given legal equality. Overnight the Revolution had brought political freedoms never before known in Russia – and hardly ever since. People could say, write, and read what they wanted, something they could not do a year later – or their great-great-grandchildren 100 years later.

Within days, scores of newspapers representing all shades of opinion began appearing on the streets of Petrograd, Moscow and other cities. There was a hunger for politics entirely unknown in Russia. A new word was coined in the language in the spring of 1917: *mittingovanie* – meaning, attending political meetings. 'Day and night, across the country, a continuous, disorderly meeting went on from February until the autumn,' observed the writer Konstantin Paustovsky, who had also seen life at the front and knew how soldiers were being politicized. In Petrograd the weeks following the February Revolution were 'a festival of liberation', wrote one foreign reporter.

> You cannot buy a hat or a packet of cigarettes without being enticed into a political discussion [...]. The servants and house porters demand advice on which party to vote for in the local elections for the Soviet. Every wall is placarded with notices of meetings, lectures [...] and announcements, not only in Russian, but in Polish, Lithuanian, Yiddish [...] Two men argue at a street corner and at once one is surrounded by an excited crowd. Even at concerts now the music is diluted with political speeches by well-known orators. The Nevsky Prospekt has become a kind of *Quartier Latin*. Book hawkers line the pavement.*

John Reed, author of one of the earliest and – despite his being so one-sided in favour of the Bolsheviks – still one of the most vivid and exciting books on the Russian Revolution, said simply that for months 'in Petrograd every street corner was a public tribune'.

* Albert Rhys Williams, *Through the Russian Revolution* (Liveright, New York, 1921).

But along with those freedoms came anarchy, violence and a breakdown in law and order which the government was unable to prevent. Immediately after the Revolution there was wild rejoicing at the fall of the Romanov monarchy. Statues of historic Tsars were torn down and imperial emblems like the double-headed eagle were destroyed amid a series of spontaneous celebrations throughout the country. They were particularly joyful in the empire beyond Russia, from Warsaw to Tiflis, where many people hoped the Revolution would soon lead to national independence. Everywhere, a republic was an overwhelmingly popular cause. Lurid, semi-pornographic, antimonarchist pamphlets with titles like *The Secrets of the Romanovs, The Night Orgies of Rasputin, The German Woman's Evil Lies* were instant bestsellers. All the institutions of the former regime were under attack.

Celebration, though, had quickly given way to something darker: a quest for revenge, which the Bolsheviks were quick to exploit, but which other socialists were convinced would destroy the ideals they had been struggling for over many decades.

Gorky had supported the 1905 insurrection and the overthrow of the Tsar but loathed the heedless 'destruction of the mob [...] an anarchic wave of plebeian violence and revenge [has] brought the country to a new dark age of barbaric chaos', he said. Other intellectuals were appalled that it was not just symbols of the old order that were being wiped out, but all traces of the past Russian civilization: national monuments, old buildings, libraries, works of art. 'This is the struggle of culture against anarchy,' Gorky said in a pessimistic piece in his newspaper, *Novaya Zhizn* (New Life).

Not everyone agreed. Alexander Blok believed that violence would be 'cleansing', a cathartic but necessary way of healing centuries-old wounds. Trotsky saw the violent mood as predictable, understandable and justifiable:

In that riotous anarchy, even in its most negative manifestations, when the soldier, yesterday's slave, all of a sudden found himself in a first-class railway carriage and tore out the velvet facings to make himself foot cloths, even in such an act of vandalism the awakening of personality was expressed. That downtrodden, persecuted Russian peasant, who was struck in the face and subjected to the vilest curses, found himself, for perhaps the first time in his life, in a first-class carriage and saw the velvet cushions, while on his feet he had stinking rags, and he tore up the velvet, saying that he too had the right to a piece of good silk or velvet.

— ★ —

FOR ALL THE hopes of people such as Nabokov, disillusion came quickly – along with the realization that the American or British political systems could not be established in Russia immediately, during a time of war. Many people, such as Zinaida Gippius in her diaries, used the same phrase or similar to describe the eight months of the Provisional Government – 'a continuing process of dying'.

From the start, there was a fatal weakness in the political arrangement immediately after the February Revolution. It has often been said that the principal problem was that two rival seats of power were established – a recipe for chaos. The Duma set up the Provisional Government first under the moderate figure of elderly Prince Lvov, who had been the decent, aristocratic, gentlemanly face of opposition to the Tsar for a generation. But on day one the government recognized the Soviet of Soldiers', Workers' and Peasants' Deputies as a partner and accepted that all government measures had to be approved by the Soviet before they were put into effect.

The soviets were hastily elected representatives from factories, army regiments and land communes, chosen within days of the

Revolution in cities, towns and villages throughout Russia. Scores of them were formed among workers of all kinds from miners to butlers via textile workers, clockmakers and waiters. They were not democratic in the modern sense; invariably they weren't elected on a secret ballot. But they were representative – up to a point. It is easy to deride the early soviets, which were more open examples of democracy than anything that had previously existed in Russia, or has existed since. They sprang from the idea that at last people could discuss things and could have a say in their lives and their work free from the ears and the control of the Okhrana. In every walk of life a soviet was formed where people could debate. There was even one among passengers of the Trans-Siberian Railway, where each carriage elected a council. This was not ideological – and early on most of the soviets were not political. On a ten-day journey the train needed to pick up large amounts of food and water and it had to be distributed fairly, so the councils were supposed to ensure that each carriage had its fair share of supplies.

The soviets were no less democratic than the Duma which appointed the coalition government; that was a gerrymandered so-called parliament rigged by the Tsar to support the Crown and based on a minuscule electorate of property owners. The Soviet and the Provisional Government were frequently at loggerheads over the next few months and both tried to claim a bogus legitimacy. It has often been said, glibly, that the Provisional Government had power without authority and the soviets had authority without power. But in fact neither had power or authority and a clever tactician like Lenin was able to expose this weakness time and again over the following months to make the system unworkable. Both the Petrograd Soviet and the Duma were based in the enormous Tauride Palace – the Soviet on the Left side and the Duma opposite.

Dmitry Moor's famous Bolshevik poster *Death to World Imperialism*. Moor became one of the most influential and best-known propagandists of the early Soviet years.

The Soviet seemed anything but a traditional chamber of parliament. 'Anyone who wants gets up and says whatever he likes,' one member said after just a couple of weeks of work.

At first [...] deputies were sitting on chairs and benches [...] and tables. In the hall stood people of every description, creating confusion and disruption. Then the crowds of standing people became so dense that it was difficult to move about in the hall. A few hours later the chairs had completely vanished [...] and people dripping with sweat stood tightly squeezed together. The next day, or the day after, the tables too had vanished, except for the chairman's and the assembly looked like a mass meeting [...] There was no time to think matters over, everything was done in haste, after many sleepless nights, in confusion. Everyone was physically exhausted. No sleep. Endless meetings. The lack of proper food; people lived on bread and tea.

The Duma was equally a madhouse – 'Members were motivated by one single characteristic: their fear of the masses – and who could blame them?' In particular, they were scared of the soldiers, whose mutiny had brought down the Tsar, and whose anger could turn on them. At first the Kadets and the Octobrists formed the majority of the new administration. They had benefited from the Revolution while taking little part in it – and they knew it. They could operate only with the acceptance of the Left. It was an uneasy relationship: 'The Revolution was made on the streets, the Government in the salons,' as Nikolai Sukhanov, one acute Menshevik journalist, pointed out.

THE 6 AGONY OF KERENSKY'S GOVERNMENT

6

THE AGONY OF KERENSKY'S GOVERNMENT

FOR SHEER POLITICAL INCOMPETENCE AND WELL-MEANING ineptitude, history has few more striking examples than the interregnum between the fall of the Tsar and the Bolshevik coup in October. Prince Lvov was a thoroughly decent, well-meaning liberal, now aged fifty-six, but entirely out of his depth in the revolutionary times of 1917. He was a rich landlord from the old nobility, with long experience of the *zemstvo* movement of local government established at the end of the previous century. He had helped to finance hundreds of hospitals, schools and agricultural colleges for peasants and had performed innumerable good works. After the serfs were emancipated, Lvov gave peasants on his estates substantially more land than the legal minimum, more generously than almost any other landlord in the country. He was a kind man but according to Nabokov, one of his closest aides, 'the very embodiment of passivity'. One of his allies, Alexander Bublikov, a powerful figure in the Duma, liked him – almost everyone liked him – but he became exasperated by Lvov's 'permanent look of dismay [...] he was a walking symbol of the Government's impotence'.

Lvov was completely over-shadowed by a charismatic younger man who took over from him as prime minister early in the summer and came to be identified with all that was wrong with the Provisional Government: Alexander Kerensky. Aged thirty-six, but looking much younger, his face was deathly pale, almost sallow, and he possessed a 'nervous, febrile manner, fragile in appearance, with a frantic intensity that made him seem to be permanently in pain.'* He was a bundle of nervous energy and tended to move his limbs jerkily in energetic bursts. The codename in his Okhrana file was 'Speedy'.

Alexander Kerensky, the leading figure of the Provisional Government which took power in February 1917. Removed by the Bolsheviks in October, Kerensky fled Russia and spent the rest of a long life in exile.

He obtained a law degree at St Petersburg University and like so many students became involved in radical politics. But he was never seduced by Marxism – he said he hated 'its austere completeness and orderly logic, borrowed from abroad' – or by revolutionary terrorism. He joined the moderate workers' group, the Trudoviks, and only later, when the war broke out, the Socialist Revolutionaries.

He was jailed for four months in the Kresty Prison during the 1905 Revolution, where his health broke down. After his release

* Nikolai Sukhanov, *The Russian Revolution 1917: A Personal Record* (Princeton University Press, Princeton, NJ, 1982).

he became a public defender in a number of high-profile political cases. He became famous for dramatic pleas for clemency against capital sentences. He was elected to the Duma in 1912 and quickly became celebrated for theatrical speeches, highly emotional, which 'left him drained [...] his whole body would tremble, sweat poured down his pale cheeks'. He was admired by the galleries, if not by the more traditional Duma members. Early in life, he had wanted to be an actor until he was persuaded to take up a more stable profession. His speeches, particularly during the war when he had a remarkable gift for rousing troops, were big set-piece occasions, occasionally accompanied by fainting fits – on the part of both speaker and audience members. A Kerensky performance, according to Gorky,

> resembled the passage of a cyclone. Crowds gathered for hours to catch a glimpse of him. His path was everywhere strewn with flowers. Soldiers ran for miles after his motor car, trying to shake his hand or kiss the hem of his garment. At his meetings in great halls [...] audiences worked themselves up into paroxysms of enthusiasm and adoration. After a speech, the platform where he had appeared would be littered with watches, rings, bracelets, military medals and bank notes, sacrificed by admirers for the common cause.

But Kerensky was not all show. He could be brave. He denounced antisemitism wherever he saw it, whether in court circles or among the lower ranks of the army. Once he went to Kuzhi (now Kuziai, in Lithuania) a small town near the front, where Jews were being lynched for allegedly helping German troops, and pleaded with soldiers and local soldiers to stop their 'barbarous and counter-productive' actions. His intervention prevented what might have turned into a far more bloody pogrom.

Kerensky was the one declared socialist in the first Provisional Government and the only one who was a member of both the Duma and the Petrograd Soviet. But he was a socialist in name only, more, as one of his friends said, 'a perpetual student radical'.* He never ventured out on the streets during the short life of the Provisional Government. He scurried between the Right and Left wings of the vast Tauride Palace trying to make himself useful, or at least plausible, to both. In the Duma he always wore a perfectly pressed morning coat with a starched dress shirt and collar. When he made fiery speeches in the Soviet he ripped off the collar and took off his coat to appear more proletarian. He was not a revolutionary, but as Trotsky said, 'a man who merely hung around the revolution'.

He presented himself after February 1917 as 'the undisputed leader of the people' and for a while his popularity was enormous. He was the favourite of the liberal intelligentsia, and also the sections of the army that wanted to continue the war. He was convinced of his own greatness, and convinced a few others too. Zinaida Gippius wrote in her diary in April, 'there is only one name that unites everybody – and that is [...] Kerensky. We loved him. There was something alive, something bird-like and childish in him. He is the right man in the right place.' The poet Marina Tsvetaeva was carried away further and compared him to Napoleon:

And someone, falling on the map,
Does not sleep in his dreams.
There came a Bonaparte
In my country.

— ★ —

* Leon Trotsky, *History of the Russian Revolution* (Scribner, New York, 1930).

Isaak Brodsky's famous portrait of Kerensky, painted in the spring of 1917.
He is wearing a soldier's uniform despite never having served in the army.

WHEN LENIN ARRIVED at the Finland Station in Petrograd on 3 April he was considered so extreme and outside the political mainstream that the government wasn't worried about him or his Bolsheviks and treated them as no real threat. That was Kerensky's first big mistake.

Lenin and his closest lieutenants had been in exile in Switzerland for a decade or more. Desperate to return to Russia after the February Revolution, the only practical way they could get back was to seek the help of Germany – hence the negotiations with the German high command to organize the famous journey of the 'sealed train' through enemy territory and Scandinavia to Petrograd. The Germans considered this an entirely reasonable strategy: if they could help stir enough political mayhem in Russia to knock one enemy out of the war they would be fighting on only one front, not two. They could transfer troops from the East to shore up their position on the Western Front.

It was a trickier dilemma for Lenin, who could be regarded as a traitor by an alliance of any sort with the Germans. He had no moral qualms about making a deal with them but knew he had to be disingenuous, keep the details quiet and carefully cover his tracks. He never felt he had to justify his actions. To him, accepting help from the Germans – and as became clear later, large amounts of their money, too – was entirely rational and reasonable. He might have argued, as Winston Churchill did twenty-five years later after making an alliance with Stalin, that 'if the devil was fighting against Hitler I'd be on the side of the devil'. Lenin by this time in his life had ceased thinking in conventional ethical terms and would have felt it entirely acceptable to take help from anyone if it would bring forward the socialist Revolution, first in Russia – and then throughout the world. But the question, whether Lenin and the Bolsheviks were 'agents' of the Germans would become a major issue in Russia later in the summer

– and has exercised historians since the USSR collapsed. Entire books have been written by Russian and Western scholars speculating whether the entire Revolution was not a German plot, arguing with convoluted logic that somehow this delegitimized it further.

The British knew about the Bolshevik leader's negotiations before the sealed train deal was agreed and Lloyd George's government considered an idea to counter the Germans by bribing Lenin to campaign for Russia to stay in the war – clearly misjudging their man and misunderstanding the stakes Lenin was playing for. They quickly dropped the suggestion.

From the moment he returned to Russia Lenin laid out a straightforward political line: there must be no compromise with other socialist groups; the Provisional Government was illegitimate; the Bolsheviks would make no deals with it or any of its supporters on the Left. He called for an immediate end to the war and 'an immediate start to building a socialist state'. For the next few months he would be more extreme, more left wing than the others, and more uncompromising than anyone. Most of the Bolshevik leadership thought he was wrong and had lost any credibility he might have possessed; some believed he had gone mad. But tactically and strategically, for the purpose of seizing power, he was right and he showed his extraordinary skill as a leader over the next six months in the way he dragged his Bolsheviks with him. At a revolutionary moment, the middle is squeezed, as Lenin often argued, leaving space for those on the extremes to emerge triumphant. That is what happened in Russia in 1917. While the Provisional Government dithered and its various supporters on the Left became increasingly unpopular, support for the Bolsheviks among workers and soldiers gradually grew. The Bolsheviks had a clear and easily understood line they repeated incessantly calling, in a simple phrase, for 'Peace, Land and Bread'.

Lenin adopted a 'modern' populist style of politics that would be recognizable – and imitated by many a rabble-rouser – 100 years later, even in long-established, sophisticated democracies. He offered simple solutions to complex problems. He was never a sparkling orator, as Kerensky and Trotsky were in their varying ways. He was not usually a charismatic speaker. But he was brilliant at presenting a case in direct, straightforward language that anyone could understand and at explaining how the world can be changed if only people would listen to him and his Bolsheviks. Economic injustice and semi-feudalism had held Russia back for centuries? His answer was simple: 'All the people have to do is expropriate a thousand banking and industrial big-shots [...] and break the resistance of a few dozen millionaires,' he said. The people were hungry for land? Simple. 'The peasants must seize the estates from their former landowner masters. They must be masters now.' Workers may not understand how to run industries? Lenin had a solution: 'Arrest a score or two of capitalists, keep them in the same condition as Nicholas Romanov now lives, and they will disclose to you all the clues and secrets of their enrichment.' Lenin knew that a revolutionary state would need experts in various fields to keep functioning. But he argued that people have heard too much from experts. 'Any worker will master any ministry in a few days; no special skill is needed.'

With brazen cynicism he would promise people everything, and anything. He promised peasants land. He didn't believe in handing the estates to peasants; he wanted to nationalize the land on which peasants would work on big state-owned collective farms. He said workers should run their factories. But he didn't actually believe in workers controlling their enterprises, or his other pledge of establishing cooperatives managed by trade unions. He aimed to centralize control of labour under the leadership of his Party. When the Provisional government delayed the Constituent Assembly elections it had originally planned for early September, Lenin attacked it for 'betraying' democracy. Of course, he didn't believe in 'bourgeois democracy', meaning free elections between competing political parties, and there would be none for seventy years in the state in which he created. He told his lieutenants that in their propaganda, 'It is important to keep things simple. We must talk about peace, land and bread, these things. Then we will shine like a beacon in the darkness.' He told what he knew were lies and justified them on the basis that he justified most things: the end – socialist revolution – justified the means.

—★—

THE PROVISIONAL GOVERNMENT drifted from crisis to crisis and always looked unstable. It survived a series of street demonstrations at the end of April which the Bolsheviks had not initiated, but which they led enthusiastically. There were more than 150,000 people on one march, many holding placards demanding 'Down With the Government', but it never got out of police control.

There were four coalitions in eight and a half months, and seven major cabinet reshuffles. None could ensure law and order, maintain a grip on the army or control inflation, which grew exponentially. The government was in no position to borrow any more from the West; its credit was worthless, so its answer was to print more money. The Treasury printing works outside Petrograd could barely keep pace – it did not have enough 'guillotines' to cut the sheets of notes from the presses, so in many cases bank customers cut off individual notes themselves. Average industrial wages trebled in the three months after February, but had fallen in real purchasing power by two-thirds.

The army was a sullen mass, defeated and depressed. Soldiers believed, with some justification, that it was their mutiny which had turned the Revolution in February and brought down the old regime. Government ministers feared the troops could do the same to them. Immediately after the Revolution the troops made a series of demands to bring 'democracy' to the army and a guarantee that they would not be prosecuted for any refusal to obey orders during the February uprising.

The deal they reached handed the Bolsheviks enormous influence within the military – especially the navy – and was a major factor in the success of their coup a few months later. Order No. 1, as it was called, had a profound effect in the armed forces. It made the army answerable to the Petrograd Soviet, not the Provisional Government; troops and sailors would elect their own committees, which would send delegates to the Soviet. Soldiers were 'citizens', not subject to martial laws. The committees would control the weapons 'which shall in no cases be surrendered to their superior officers'. They would no longer have to salute officers when they were off duty; officers were banned from striking the men, as they habitually had in the Tsarist army. Officers had to address their men with the formal 'vy' rather than the 'ty' reserved for children and servants. Soldiers addressed their officers as 'Mr General' or 'Mr Colonel' rather than 'Your Honour' or 'Your Excellency'.

The Bolsheviks despatched a large number of recruiting sergeants into the barracks; soldiers were joining the Party en masse. 'This is the end of the army,' declared the influential reactionary politician Vasily Shulgin when he heard about Order No. 1.

But the army was already dead. More than a million and a quarter men had already deserted – around 10,000 a day left their regiments in April and May. 'All discipline has vanished in the army,' Colonel Alfred Knox, Britain's military attaché to Russia reported back to London.

A committee of soldiers from the front meet in Petrograd. Order No. 1 of the Petrograd Soviet made the Russian army answerable to that body, and gave solders the right to send delegates to it.

Officers are being insulted [...] and if they complain are massacred [...] Deserters are wandering over Russia, filling the stations, storming the carriages and paralysing the transport links, both military and civil. Soldiers positively swarm at big junctions. A train arrives: the soldiers make the passengers get out, take their places and compel the station master to switch the train's destination to wherever they demand.

The government had ceased counting the number of deserters and even if they caught up with some of them, 'What could we do?' wondered General Vladislav Klembovski, an aide to the chiefs of staff at army headquarters. 'The death sentence? You can't hang whole divisions. Courts martial? But then half the army will be in Siberia. You don't frighten soldiers with the threat of imprisonment or hard labour. "What of it. We will be back in five years – with a whole skin," they say.'

Troops had become radicalized, but not necessarily in the way the Bolsheviks wanted. General Brusilov, who would be appointed Army Chief in the summer of 1917, said later that:

The soldiers wanted one thing: peace – so they could go home [to their villages], rob the landowners and live freely without paying taxes or recognize any authority. Soldiers veered towards Bolshevism because they believed it was their programme. They did not have the slightest idea of what Communism was, or what the socialist International meant, but they imagined themselves at home, living without laws or landowners. The anarchistic 'freedom' is what they called Bolshevism.

The writer Ivan Bunin spent the first part of 1917 in a village on the Volga and kept a brilliant diary of the period. He was a vitriolic anti-

Bolshevik, but he agreed with Lenin about the war. The peasants were simply fed up with the conflict and 'realized, as their masters should have, that victory was impossible [...] The people don't want to fight. They are tired of the war and they don't understand what we are fighting for. The war isn't their business. They grow more furious by the day.'

Lenin's critics were appalled at his determination to stir up class hatreds for his political ends. But to him, socialism *was* class war; and the accompanying violence was 'the inevitable result'. Chaos in Russia, he told close comrades, should be welcomed on the basis that 'what's bad for them, the bourgeois government, is good for us'. But even some of his admirers were shocked by the crude, mob-rousing populism he displayed in the spring and summer of 1917, such as the slogan he used in most speeches 'Loot the looters.' The passionate socialist Gorky was in despair. 'Every day my anxiety grows,' he wrote to his wife on 14 June. 'The crazy politics of Lenin will soon lead to a civil war.'

—★—

WAR WAS already happening on the land. The Provisional Government's writ never ran throughout much of provincial Russia, where law and order had entirely broken down. Hundreds of large estates were seized by peasants who evicted, brutalized and in many cases murdered their landowners. It was a process that began well before the Bolshevik seizure of power, almost immediately after the February Revolution. The 'march[es] on the manors' were spontaneous, though often played out in similar ways. First, peasants went on rent strikes, boycotted working for the landowner and made demands like the forced sale of grain and livestock to the commune at 'fair' prices. In the past the squire was protected by the army, which for centuries had put down peasant unrest using harsh measures. But since the Revolution, the soldiers were often the instigators of the violence and in many parts of the country the police no longer existed. The squire was now on his own.

Fury against the estate owners had been an abiding tradition among the *muzhiks*. Deep within the commune – the *mir* – under serfdom was the belief that land should not be privately owned by the gentry who never worked on it, but only by those who ploughed the fields and tended the livestock. 'We are yours, but the land is ours,' the saying went. The accepted belief was that one day the Tsar would divide up the land anew and hand over the estates to peasant farmers in an entirely new dispensation. The Tsar was gone, but now, many thought, was the chance for the great redivision of the land that would bring justice for the peasantry. From the early summer, mostly in areas with the best agricultural land, peasants would meet in villages and vote to confiscate the squire's domains. Groups of men – there were some women, but mostly it was men with guns, pitchforks and hoes – would head for the manor, demand to see the landlord, and evict the whole family, usually with just hours' notice.

Often the process was accompanied by violence, justified as payback for the brutality of the period of 1905–07, when thousands of peasants were killed by soldiers acting on behalf of the gentry landowners. In early June 1917 at the fine manor house of Bor-Polianshcina near Saratov, a mob led by a group of army deserters, hacked the aged Prince Vladimir Saburov to death with axes as retribution for the role his son had played as local 'land captain' in 1906 when twelve peasants had been hanged in front of their wives and children. After the bloody murder they burned down the house, which had been home to one of the finest private libraries in Europe.

They marched on Tolstoy's manor at Yasnaya Polyana, 125 miles south of Moscow, despite the fact that the great novelist had idolized the Russian peasantry and always campaigned for their rights. His aged and half-blind widow, Sonia, pleaded for help from the Provisional Government, but none came. She and her daughters packed her books and boxes in one room and stood guard with a revolver and an axe. On the night the mob came to the manor all the lights were off and they assumed the house had already been looted, so they passed on to another estate nearby.

At the end of May a newly created All-Russian Assembly of Peasants, a self-appointed group of delegates from local land assemblies, declared that all the property seizures that had been carried out so far were legal, and all their so-called 'laws' were legitimate. The Bolsheviks supported the organization on the basis that they would promise the peasants anything to gain their backing. But it was a charade. The Marxist Left had a low opinion of Russia's *muzhiks*, who they regarded as barbaric and semi-feudal. Nevertheless they went along with the assemblies – for now. As the Bolshevik leader in Nizhny Novgorod said, barely disguising his contempt, 'The local peasantry has [...] a fixed opinion that all civil laws have lost their force [since February] and that all legal relations ought now to be regulated by peasant organizations.'

Prince Boris Vyazemsky refused to accept the verdict of one of these assemblies that he must hand over Lotarevo, his family estate in the fertile Tambov 'Black Earth' province in central Russia, with its beautiful manor house, stud farm and hospital. His brother Dmitri had been among the most brutal of the army officers who had hanged hundreds of peasants in the troubles of 1906, and the entire family had been resented since. When a mob came to evict him with sticks and clubs in the summer of 1917 a village elder said that though they respected him personally they wanted to finish for good with the Vyazemskys and 'take the land that rightfully belongs to us'. The

Some of the greatest artists of the age were enthusiastically behind the
Revolution – at the beginning. Kazimir Malevich's *Head of a Peasant*
was one of many propaganda posters he produced for the Bolsheviks.

peasants formed a kangaroo court and ordered him to be sent to the war front. He had barely got to the nearest railway station before another mob of army deserters and peasants ran him through with bayonets. When he was dead they cut off his head.

The peasants had made their own revolution – before the Bolsheviks would later unmake it for them and impose their own version of what a revolution should be.

—★—

THE PROVISIONAL GOVERNMENT'S second big mistake – after underestimating the Bolsheviks – was to continue with the war. Lenin told comrades in the Party several times in May and June that the one thing he really feared was that Kerensky would 'do the sensible thing', steal Bolshevik policy and seek a separate peace with Germany. He could not understand why they had not done so. 'It would cut the ground from under our feet,' he told Trotsky at the beginning of June. The Western Allies were exerting pressure on Kerensky – whose title was War Minister, but who was in effect head of the government – to stick with the war effort, but as one of the British diplomats sent to Petrograd to stiffen the war-weary Russians' resolve admitted, it was futile and, worse, counterproductive. 'The Allies were blinded [...] and entirely failed to see what was possible and what was not,' the British espionage agent Robert Bruce Lockhart wrote later. 'They were simply playing into Lenin's hands and estranging the Kerensky government from the Russian people.' It was a woefully short-sighted policy, a boon to the Bolsheviks, led directly to a military disaster that hastened the second 1917 Revolution and helped to bring about the outcome they least wanted: the Bolsheviks in power and Russian withdrawal from the war.

Kerensky thought about reaching an armistice with Germany but he ruled it out. Instead, he and the principal Kadet ministers did the opposite and tried to show the Allies a further commitment to the war. They persuaded the generals to lay plans for a summer offensive – a big push that would drive the Germans and Austrians out of Ukraine, much of which had been occupied for two years. Before it began, the army chief of staff, Brusilov, warned Kerensky of his growing doubts. Dozens of mutinies had already taken place even in supposedly loyal and well-trained units, and thousands of soldiers were refusing to move up to the front. As many as three-quarters of the troops might desert, he told Kerensky – 'But he paid not the slightest attention to my words.'

The offensive was a desperate gamble, with odds stacked against the Russians. On 16 June came the so-called 'final push' with a two-day heavy artillery bombardment of German trenches in north-west Ukraine. Two days later the troops moved forward and at first the German lines were broken – a 'Triumph for Liberty' was heralded in the patriotic newspapers. But the advance stalled on the third day; the Germans regrouped and counterattacked. The Russians fled in panic. The supply lines were stretched and many units were without weapons or ammunition. But the main reason the offensive failed was that the men refused to fight. In one night alone, a crack battalion of the 11th Army arrested 12,000 deserters near the Ukrainian town of Volochysk. There were hundreds of instances of men shooting their officers before running away.

The Russians lost nearly 200,000 men killed or wounded and millions of square miles of territory in a few weeks. Baron Alexei Budberg, from a famous noble family, was a colonel in one of the frontline regiments and anything but a typical, reactionary old-school officer. He said that even before this point the army 'no longer existed as a military organization […] 80 per cent of the soldiers, officers and men, would have agreed with the slogan "Down with the War." It's terrible as an officer, to give an order without any confidence – often without the slightest hope – that it will be carried out.' The failed offensive was a fatal blow for the Provisional Government and the authority of its leaders – and a big boost for the Bolsheviks.

THE SPOILS
OF WAR

7

7

THE SPOILS OF WAR

THE PROVISIONAL GOVERNMENT WAS TOTTERING, ASSAILED BY the extremes of the Left and Right. If after the failure of the summer offensive in the war it had called immediate elections for a constituent assembly – as was promised after the Revolution in February – it might have claimed some belated legitimacy. But the vote was repeatedly postponed – a propaganda coup for the Bolsheviks and a political problem for the other socialist groups which supported the government. But when Kerensky officially took over as premier he put off the elections until November at the earliest. For most of his time in office, he ruled effectively by decree, with a five-man Directory comprising two generals, one obscure Menshevik and the former Finance Minister Mikhail Tereshchenko, a multimillionaire industrial oligarch. This was not democracy, and the government's inability to maintain any kind of law and order or to control inflation drove increasing numbers of people further to the extremes. The country faced anarchy. The sense of chaos and drift turned even some of Kerensky's chief admirers from the intelligentsia against him, people like the theatre director Konstantin Stanislavsky, the poet Marina Tsvetaeva, and the writer Dmitri Merezhovsky, whose wife Zinaida Gippius wrote in her diary in the summer: 'Exactly when the slaughter, the cannonades, the uprising, the pogrom in St Petersburg will start is still uncertain. But it will come.'

Kerensky possessed no real power. His government was just about surviving day to day. He was in many ways a decent man, unable to control the great sweep of events unfolding in Russia. But his real weakness was vanity: the appearance of power went to his head. When he became Premier, he signalled that he was aiming to sideline the Petrograd Soviet by moving it to the Smolny Institute. The government returned to the traditional seat of administration, the Winter Palace, where he began to live, taking over the former suite of Alexander III. He slept in the late Tsar's bed. He had a picture taken of himself behind Alexander's immense desk, which he sent to admirers. He had Nicholas II's billiard table, which had been in a packing case since the abdication, placed back in one of the state rooms. When he came and went the flag on the Palace roof was raised and lowered, as it had been for the Tsars.

Meanwhile, in reality, each coalition the Provisional Government formed was weaker than the last, the food queues were getting longer, crime on the streets was an epidemic – 'government has come to a standstill at the top and locally,' wrote Sukhanov, whose first-hand eyewitness account of the Revolution is still an invaluable source. Inflation was climbing dangerously. The government was printing money at an unprecedented rate – 429 million paper roubles in April, 729 million in June, 1.1 billion in July. Prices of some basic foodstuffs had quadrupled between February and the end of July. More than 500 factories in Petrograd and Moscow had closed down and over 100,000 workers had lost their jobs in the capital in the five months after February. The economy had ground to a near halt.

—★—

THE BOLSHEVIKS were emboldened by a dramatic increase in their membership – and by the availability of a vast source of funds. From a maximum of around 20,000 members at the beginning of March, the membership had reached about 250,000 by July, still far fewer than the Social Revolutionaries and the Mensheviks, but a growing force in the army (and especially the navy). They were a major power on an increasing number of factory floors by the summer. More important, the Bolsheviks had quickly established a thriving newspaper empire – by far the largest of any other political organization in the country. *Pravda* was legalized at the end of February. By mid-April it was printing – and selling – 85,000 copies a day in Petrograd. There were provincial editions of the paper and versions for different nationalities which appeared in Georgian, Latvian, Polish, Armenian and Yiddish. Large editions were produced for soldiers – *Soldatskavie Pravda* for front-line troops had a daily print run of 70,000 – and a special edition for sailors. Suddenly the Bolsheviks were able to afford a brand-new, expensive, printing press, and had the money for large stocks of newsprint, a distribution system involving large numbers of people and they found competent journalists to produce readable, in some cases brilliant, copy. Altogether, by the beginning of July, they were producing forty-one publications with a circulation of nearly 350,000 copies a day. 'It was an extraordinary feat of organization' to get the papers up and running so quickly, said Trotsky, and it made a huge propaganda impact for the Bolsheviks. People who had barely heard of them before now knew where they stood – certainly on the issue of the war. The money had come mostly, though not entirely, from the Germans as part of the 'sealed train' deal, via a circuitous route involving a variety of intermediaries in an effort to hide its origins.

Few Bolsheviks outside the small circle close to Lenin knew the details of the arrangement and there is no paper trail linking the

Party directly to any transaction with the Germans. It was some time after the Soviet Union collapsed in 1991 before any firm evidence came to light; the Communists carefully buried the proof for more than seventy years. Even now the details are sketchy. Nobody knows for sure how much money was funnelled from Germany to the Bolsheviks between February 1917 until at least March 1918 but the suggestion from Kerensky that it was the equivalent of scores of millions of US dollars is wide of the mark. Whatever the figure it was certainly a large sum.

The Germans admitted later that they backed the Bolsheviks financially, without saying by how much. They congratulated themselves on a successful strategy when the Bolsheviks took power. The German Minister for Foreign Affairs Richard von Kühlmann was almost inclined to boast. 'It was not until the Bolsheviks had received from us a steady flow of funds through various channels and under different labels, that they were in a position to build up their organ, *Pravda*, to conduct energetic propaganda and appreciably to extend the narrow base of their Party [...] It is entirely in our interests,' he said.

A big war chest from Germany was a boost to Bolshevik fortunes. But the incompetence of their opponents was a bigger factor – and Lenin was quick to seize the opportunities they repeatedly gave him. After the disaster of the failed summer offensive the Bolsheviks benefited from the clear anti-war line they had held since Lenin had returned from exile. It had seemed reckless at first, as it could be presented as unpatriotic. But the consistency of the message 'shone with a bright and simple clarity', as even one of the Bolsheviks' chief critics, the Kadet leader Pavel Milyukov, admitted later – although he was a much more distinguished historian and writer than politician.

The other enormous boost to the Bolsheviks came in mid-May with the arrival back in Russia of Leon Trotsky from exile in New York.

Close collaborators for a while in the late 1890s, he had parted ways with Lenin in the Party schism between Bolsheviks and Mensheviks in 1902. The two had spent the best part of fifteen years abusing each other in print and at various socialist conferences. But now Trotsky threw in his lot with the Bolsheviks, calculating that if a socialist revolution was going to happen in Russia the Bolsheviks offered the only plausible path to power. From now until Lenin's death there were hardly any significant political differences between them and for the period until the October Revolution Trotsky's was the public face of the Bolsheviks. He was far better known than Lenin inside Russia and hugely enjoyed the limelight – 'While Lenin needed an office, Trotsky needed a stage,' it was said. Trotsky appeared several nights a week to full houses at the enormous Cirque Moderne on the outskirts of Petrograd, which seated around 3,700 people. He fascinated and terrified the middle classes – 'The very incarnation of the revolutionary [...] his huge forehead surmounted by great masses of black wavy hair [...] lips heavy and protruding [...] he was all temperament, an individual artist,' according to Sukhanov, who loathed and admired him. He caused a sensation. He had a sharp, somewhat rasping, high-pitched voice. But on his day he was a brilliant performer – funny, direct, imaginative and inspiring. One eyewitness, a Menshevik who went from curiosity, was among listeners at Trotsky's first appearance after his return from exile.

The mood was one of excitement throughout the hall. The hush of the audience indicated expectation. They (were) mainly soldiers and workers, though the crowd consisted of a few bourgeois, male and female. Trotsky at once began to heat up the atmosphere [...] He depicted with extraordinary force the suffering of soldiers in the trenches [...] Trotsky knew what he was doing. Soviet power, he said, was destined not only to put an end to the suffering of the soldiers at the front. It would provide land and stop internal disorder. 'The Soviet government will give everything the country has to the poor and to the soldiers. You, bourgeois,' he would point to the well-dressed people in pricier seats. 'You own two coats? Give one to the soldier freezing in the trenches. You have warm boots? Stay at home. Your boots are needed by a worker.' It seemed that the mob would at any moment, spontaneously burst into some kind of religious hymn. 'We will defend the cause of the workers and peasants to the last drop of our blood,' he said. 'Who is in favour?' The crowd [...] raised its hands as one. I saw the uplifted hands and burning eyes of men, women, adolescents, workers, soldiers, peasants. They agreed. They vowed. I watched this truly grandiose spectacle with an unusually heavy heart.

— ★ —

FOR ALL LENIN's tactical acumen and Trotsky's flamboyant appeal, and their growing support, the Bolsheviks made serious missteps. The gravest became known as the 'July Days' (the 4th and 5th). The Bolsheviks had called for a series of anti-war and anti-government demonstrations in Petrograd. The demonstrations turned violent and there were bloody clashes in the streets. The city was in chaos. Kerensky, the Kadets and even some Bolsheviks and their sympathizers thought an attempted coup was taking place. Sergo Ordzhonikidze, a leading Party organizer, and at that time a close friend of Stalin – he would later become the leader of the Bolsheviks in Georgia – said he believed the demonstration was 'the first serious attempt to finish with the power of the Provisional Government'. Others were not so sure, including most of the Menshevik leadership and the Provisional Government's chief intelligence official, Boris Nikitin, who admitted that it was more of a 'muddle than a plot'.

Even now the only thing that is clear about the July Days is that there was nothing planned or organized about them. Revisionist historians are mostly agreed that it was a putsch attempt. But no account on those lines seems convincing. For a start, Lenin was taking a 'holiday' at the time at a house by a lake in a remote part of Finland. It is highly unlikely that he would have authorized an insurrection if he was not in Petrograd to oversee it. Lenin had dreamed of a revolution for most of his life, had written about little else for twenty-five years, had made himself an expert on 'the art' of insurrection. Surely, if this was the central moment of his life, when he would take power in Russia, he wouldn't have left things so much to chance. It seems entirely out of character.

On the other hand, the Bolsheviks had called for the demon-strations and it was always probable that they could get out of

Rioters on Nevsky Prospect, St Petersburg, early July 1917, photographed by Viktor Bulla. The riot left dozens dead and resulted in the arrest of some fifty Bolshevik activists, including Trotsky.

control. They appeared to want their cake and to eat it. When the rioting began while Lenin was 'on vacation' the leadership left in Petrograd panicked, had no idea what to do and lost their nerve.

Some military units – the 1st Rifle Brigade and a large contingent of sailors from the Kronstadt naval base – mutinied, pledged loyalty to the Bolsheviks, and wanted to storm the Tauride Palace to topple the government and the Duma. For several hours on 3 July they were in control of Petrograd and could easily have marched into the Tauride and the Winter Palace if they had wanted to. The Bolshevik leadership dithered and never gave the order and then tried – too late – to call off the demonstrations.

Later in the day troops loyal to the government fought back. Around 300 people – soldiers and civilians – died in street battles. The city was in total confusion. Nobody knew who was in charge of the government; Kerensky was in Kyiv following a series of fiery speeches to troops on the Ukraine front. Angry soldiers from both sides were patrolling the streets, where isolated rioting continued all day. Sailors and troops backing the Bolsheviks couldn't understand why the Party bosses hadn't seized power when it looked as though it was theirs. Lenin rushed back to Petrograd from Finland on an overnight train and, humiliated, tried to explain. Those present thought it was one of the worst speeches of his life, full of half apologies and weasel words. There had been no plot to overthrow the government: 'It was a little more than a demonstration, but a lot less than an insurrection,' he said, which convinced very few. The next day a warrant was issued for his arrest on charges of treason and the press was full of stories about his financial dealings with the Germans. Fearing for his life, Lenin escaped back to Finland. A score of leading Bolsheviks were jailed, including Trotsky and some of Lenin's closest lieutenants.

July 1917: Red Guards training at a firing range in the aftermath of the July Days.

Lenin was in hiding for the next three months. He genuinely feared being killed if he stayed in Petrograd. 'This is when they are going to shoot us,' he told an associate. 'It would be the most advantageous time for them.' This wasn't paranoia, but an accurate judgement of his value to the Revolution he intended to lead. Trotsky was clear. 'If they (the Provisional Government) had managed to arrest him it is likely they would have dealt with him in the manner the German army officers dealt with Rosa Luxemburg,' he wrote later.* 'In that case it is very probable there wouldn't have been a Bolshevik revolution.' A bitter ideological enemy, the American Ambassador to Russia, David R. Francis, made the same point and had continually advised the government to arrest Lenin. 'Had the Provisional Government [...] tried and executed him Russia would not have been compelled to go through another Revolution, would have been spared the reign of terror and the loss from famine and murder of millions of her sons and daughters,' he wrote.

—★—

LATER IN THE summer the hate campaign in the press against Lenin and the 'traitor Bolsheviks' reached a crescendo. Newspaper cartoons depicted Lenin on the gallows (though one of the first things the Provisional Government had done was to abolish the death penalty). In the press he was public enemy number one. But in reality the police were only going through the motions of searching for him; most of the 800 or so 'subversives' arrested after the July riots were freed within a few weeks. Kerensky was far less worried about the Bolsheviks

---

* In Germany, following the left-wing Spartacist Uprising of January 1919, the revolutionary socialist Rosa Luxemburg was shot by right-wing *Freikorps* paramilitaries and her body thrown in a canal.

than by threats from the Right. The Kadets, some monarchists and reactionary newspapers were demanding 'an end to anarchy' and he feared a counterrevolution led by the army.

Kerensky believed that the Right was planning a coup to install as dictator the popular general Lavr Kornilov, a genuine war hero from the early days of the fighting in 1914–15 and, since the February Revolution, commander of the Petrograd Military District. There are various interpretations of the so-called Kornilov Affair; even now, many still cling to the view held by generations of Soviet historians that the general had ambitions to be a dictator. But, like the July Days, the story is murky. It is highly probable that Kornilov was never planning to topple the government, but wanted to force Kerensky to act more firmly against the Bolsheviks and the other socialist groups to bypass the Soviet – 'a council of rats and dogs' as he called it. Yet Kerensky saw him as a serious rival and the old Right as a real threat.

Kornilov, a wiry, forty-seven-year-old Cossack, was politically naïve and not the most intelligent of operators – 'He has the heart of a lion, but the brains of a sheep,' according to his former army commander, General Alexeev. He had surrounded himself with a group of pro-monarchy advisors and oddball charlatans, who were using him in their own power play. When in mid-August Kornilov made a series of political demands to toughen Kerensky against the Left, the prime minister seized his opportunity and plotted the general's downfall. He accused Kornilov of mounting a coup attempt, fabricated the evidence to 'prove' it, and ordered the general's arrest on treason charges. Foolishly, Kornilov reacted by declaring martial law and sending troops to Petrograd to 'support the government and stiffen its resolve'. Was this a mutiny or a bid to give Kerensky a helping hand against anarchy? Kerensky appealed to the Left – the Bolsheviks,

Top: Lenin speaking at a rally in the summer of 1917.
Trotsky can clearly be seen just below the lectern on the right.

Above: The Communist theory of history. The same picture
reproduced a few years later in the Stalin era. Trotsky has
been airbrushed out.

Mensheviks and SRs – for help and the Bolsheviks enthusiastically answered the call.

The so-called Kornilov 'coup' was over without a shot being fired; loyal troops found the general, arrested and jailed him. But Bolshevik mythmaking for the next seven decades claimed that they had been the decisive factor in defeating it. They had sent a few Red Guards to mount a defence of the Winter Palace if need be, but they were never called upon. They manned some road blocks. That was the extent of their militant action. Yet the Kornilov Affair turned into a propaganda victory for Lenin, who masterfully spun it to appear that he had 'halted' a counterrevolution and the return of the Tsar. It was yet another disaster for Kerensky. Now he was totally isolated. The Right and moderate liberals didn't trust him. They saw him as weak. The Left mocked him. 'Kerensky personified the accidental,' said Trotsky. 'His best speeches were mainly a sumptuous pounding of water in a mortar. In 1917 the water boiled and sent up steam – and the clouds provided a halo.'

'‘INSURRECTION IS AN ART’

8

8

'INSURRECTION IS AN ART'

FROM MID-SEPTEMBER LENIN BECAME CONVINCED THAT THE time to strike against the Provisional Government would be soon and if the Bolsheviks missed their chance another might not come again – maybe for years. He still believed Kerensky could make a peace deal with the Germans, or move the government to Moscow, a move that would have made mounting an insurrection much more difficult. If he had been in Kerensky's position that is exactly what he would have done, he said later. At the start of the month the Bolsheviks won small majorities on both the Petrograd and Moscow Soviets – 'a big advance that will mean a lot,' said Trotsky. Again, as in 1905, he became chairman and public face of the Petrograd Soviet. From now the Bolsheviks' demand of 'All Power to the Soviets' became more strident.

Since going into hiding in Finland, Lenin had moved around constantly, by the lakes, in small villages, and for three weeks in the capital city Helsingfors (now Helsinki), staying in the house of an ardent Bolshevik, who also happened to be the city's chief of police. From his various Finnish hideouts he wrote a series of ever-more desperate letters to the comrades in Petrograd, demanding insurrection – now. On 12 September: 'We must at once begin to

The only known picture of Lenin without his trademark beard, which he had shaved off to escape arrest in St Petersburg. The photo was taken when he was on the run in Finland, in the summer of 1917.

plan the practical details of a second revolution. The majorities [on the soviets] show that people are with us if we immediately promise bread, peace and land.'

The next day he was more shrill:

There is no reason to wait for events such as the Congress of Soviets [scheduled for 25 October]. To wait is lunacy for the Congress will do nothing. It cannot do anything. First, we must beat Kerensky, then convene the Congress. As Marx said, insurrection is an art [...] It would be naïve to wait for a formal majority for the Bolsheviks [...] History will never forgive us if we do not take power now.

The other Bolsheviks in the leadership were stunned. Almost none of them believed they had the strength to pull off a coup; some believed they should share power with the other socialist parties; most believed that organizing a violent takeover that failed would result in 'us being hanged from lamp posts,' as one of the longest-serving of Lenin's lieutenants, the usually ultra-loyal Grigory Zinoviev said. They decided to burn every copy of the letters – except one. During Lenin's absence, the rest of the Party leadership had been following a more conciliatory line. They had even taken part in joint meetings with Kerensky's aides to work out legislation for the long planned Constituent Assembly elections. If the government or the Kadets had obtained evidence that Lenin was planning an imminent coup they could destroy the Bolsheviks.

The next few weeks showed Lenin's great skills as a leader and a tactician and disproves Marx's points about the minor importance of individuals and character in making history. He dragged his reluctant and frightened comrades with him towards an uprising most of them did not want. He used a mixture of guile, logic, bluster, threats and calmer persuasion to impose his will on them. Without Lenin driving them, hectoring them, most of the others would have been 'content just talking about Revolution', said Trotsky.

He tried one more time towards the end of September with another 'letter from afar' as he called it.

> The Bolsheviks are *guaranteed* victory in an uprising [...] if we *suddenly* strike from three points: Piter [Petrograd], Moscow and the Baltic fleet. We have the technical capability and the armed support. If we seize the Winter Palace, the General Staff, the telephone exchanges, the railway stations [...] it is 99 per cent certain that we will win with few losses [...] it is my profound belief that if we wait and let the present moment pass, we shall *ruin* the Revolution.

He told comrades in the leadership that if they didn't approve his plan he would resign from the Central Committee and take his ideas 'to the membership'. That threat made them think again. At the same time he demanded that they let him go back to Petrograd so he could lead them in person. They refused. His safety was too important, they told him. But he defied them and, with the help of the Helsingfors police chief, disguised himself as a Lutheran pastor, bought a wig to cover his now familiar bald pate, and – telling almost no one outside his family of his movements – secretly returned to the city. He demanded an immediate showdown with the other Bolshevik powerbrokers in the Party's Central Committee.

—★—

AT 10 P.M. ON WEDNESDAY 10 October – still in a dog-collar, disguised as a priest – Lenin arrived at a smart Petrograd apartment block, 32 Karpovka, overlooking the Neva. He knew the third-floor flat he was about to visit would be safe: it was the home of the prominent Menshevik journalist, and a strong critic of the Bolsheviks, Nikolai Sukhanov; this was the last place Kerensky's spies would think to look for him. Sukhanov's wife Galina Flakserman, however, was a Bolshevik and had suggested to her husband, affectionately, that perhaps that night he should sleep somewhere near his office, as he occasionally did, rather than make the tiresome six-mile journey at night when the tram service was unreliable.

History can be dramatic and full of exciting, rousing action on battlefields and at the barricades – and sometimes it can be made in committee meetings. There were twenty-one Bolshevik Central Committee members, but only twelve sat at the round table beneath a single lamp in Sukhanov's living room where the decision was made to trigger the Russian Revolution. It was a minority of an already very small minority.

Lenin spoke for an hour and repeated his demands that a coup should be mounted immediately. He was impatient and constantly on the verge of anger but as Trotsky said later, 'he was obviously restraining himself.'

Occasionally he banged his fist on the table to emphasize a point. 'Since the beginning of September there has been a certain indifference to the idea of insurrection,' he began. Then he outlined clearly and in detail why 'we must seize power now and not wait for the Soviets, or any Congresses [...] The time is right [...] The success of the Russian and the world Revolution depends on two or three days' struggle.' The arguments ran on for seven and a half hours. At first the leader was in a minority, but overnight he won the doubters around.

Only Lenin's oldest comrades Zinoviev and Boris Kamenev held out to the end. They were against a coup on principle and for practical reasons. 'There is no demand by the people for an uprising,' said Kamenev. There was everything to be gained by 'waiting a few weeks for the Constituent Assembly where we have an excellent chance of winning a big legal majority. Comrade Lenin's plan means to stake on one card the fate not only of our Party, but the fate of the Russian and world Revolution.'

Almost at dawn a vote was taken. It went Lenin's way 10–2, with only Zinoviev and Kamenev against. Lenin reached across the table and picked up a pencil. There was no paper so – famously – he scrawled on a child's exercise book the biggest decision the Bolsheviks ever took: 'Recognizing that an armed uprising is inevitable and the time perfectly ripe, the Central Committee proposes to all the organizations of the Party to act accordingly and to discuss and decide from this point of view all the practical questions.'

—★—

IT WAS THE WORST-kept 'secret' plot in history, a slow-motion putsch everyone knew was coming. Kamenev and Zinoviev went public with their opposition the following day. They distributed to Party members in Petrograd an address that stated: 'Before history, before the international proletariat, before the Russian revolution and the Russian working class, we have no right to stake the whole future at the present moment upon the card of armed insurrection.'

All of Petrograd was talking about an imminent coup. Gorky's newspaper *Novaya Zhizn* speculated on the date, predicting, almost correctly, 20 October. The Kadet paper *Resch* (Speak) under the headline 'Anarchy' called the date right: 25 October. Kerensky was as out of touch and complacent as the Tsar had been; he told the British Ambassador, Sir George Buchanan, a few days before the uprising, 'All I want them to do is act [...] then I will crush them.' On 20 October he told Nabokov that if and when the insurrection began it would 'be like July again [...] I am prepared to offer prayers for a rebellion. I have greater forces than necessary. They will be utterly defeated.' On 21 October, after speaking to Kerensky, the American Ambassador Francis cabled the State Department. 'Beginning to think the Bolsheviks will make no demonstrations; if so shall regret as believe sentiment is turning against them and [now is an] opportune moment for giving them wholesome lesson.' Some leading personalities on the far Right relished a coup. The steel and metals industrialist Stepan Lianozov – 'The Russian Rockefeller' in the popular press – told John Reed that a Bolshevik insurrection would not last a day. 'The government would declare a state of siege [...] the military commanders can deal with those gentlemen without legal formalities.'

But the government made no effort to prevent the coup. They made no arrests of Bolsheviks. They didn't try to seize Bolshevik headquarters at the Smolny. They didn't reinforce the defences of the Neva bridges or any communications centres. They didn't believe the Bolsheviks could win.

Trotsky, officially named head of the Bolsheviks' Military Revolutionary Committee on 12 October, made little secret about what it was up to. One of the first things it did was to issue a public 'mission statement' – rather strange for a conspiratorial revolutionary group about to plot a revolutionary insurrection. 'In the interests of the defence of the revolution and its conquests against attacks by counterrevolution, commissars have been appointed by us in military units and at strategic points in the capital and its environs.'

On 21 October he made one of his most dramatic appearances at the Cirque Moderne. He whipped the audience into a near-frenzy. After a fiery speech he demanded: 'If you support us without hesitation [...] and want to bring the Revolution to victory, if you give the cause all your strength [...] let us all swear our allegiance to the Revolution. If you support this sacred oath we are making then raise your hands.' The entire audience rose and shouted 'We swear.'

Kerensky was now loathed by the people who had idolized him a few months earlier. On 24 October, the eve of the Revolution, Zinaida Gippius wrote in her diary, 'Nobody wants the Bolsheviks. But nobody is prepared to fight for Kerensky either.'

A 9
DISORDERLY
COUP

9

A DISORDERLY COUP

It is an enduring myth that the Russian Revolution was an impeccably organized operation by a group of highly disciplined conspirators who knew exactly what they were doing throughout. It is a version of events that suited both sides. Soviet historians in the following decades presented 'glorious October' as a rising of the masses, brilliantly led by the master of timing and tactics, V. I. Lenin, and his skilful, heroic lieutenants in the Bolshevik Party, who kept to a strict timetable of insurrection.

The defeated 'Whites', as they would soon be called, also held to a comforting myth: that they lost power in a precisely calibrated military takeover masterminded by an evil genius with diabolical plans. It would not have impressed the loyalists' supporters – or soothed their own *amour-propre* – if it was put about that they were beaten by a group of plotters who very nearly botched their revolution. The Bolsheviks might easily have failed if at certain key moments they had met some slight resistance.

In reality the supposedly perfect clockwork timekeeping of the insurrection was so vague that nobody could tell for certain exactly when the rising began. At one stage the Mayor of Petrograd sent a delegation to the participants of both sides wondering if the insurrection had begun.

He could get no accurate answer. The Bolsheviks had little military experience. They failed to master the Petrograd telephone system and had to send runners throughout the city streets. The key force of sailors from the Kronstadt naval base – reliable Bolshevik supporters – arrived in Petrograd a day late. Most historians use the word 'coup' to describe the October Revolution, as I have done here as shorthand. But that suggests there was a takeover of a working government. By this stage the government had long ago ceased to function. 'Power was on the streets; we took it,' as Trotsky wrote later.

The Bolsheviks won because the Provisional Government under Kerensky was even more incompetent and divided, and because they didn't take the Bolsheviks seriously until it was too late. But mainly it was because most of the people didn't care which side won.

The storming of the Winter Palace, as seen in Sergei Eisenstein's film *October* (1928). Many more people were hired as extras for the movie than took part in the real events.

Overnight on 24–25 October small groups of Red Guards seized the strategic command positions of the city. They secured all the bridges across the Neva before dawn, except for the Nikolai Bridge next to the Winter Palace. Earlier they had captured the Peter and Paul Fortress, directly across the river, whose guns held a commanding view of the Palace. The occasional crack of gunfire could be heard, but there had been no serious fighting. 'It happened while the city was in deep slumber,' recorded Sukhanov. 'More like the changing of the guard than an insurrection.' At 6 a.m. the State Bank fell, an hour later the Central Telephone Exchange, the main Post Office and the Telegraph Building. By 8 a.m. the rebels had taken all the railway stations. The Bolsheviks controlled communications throughout Petrograd and had barely fired a shot. There were no casualties. In theory the government could call on the city's garrison troops, numbering some 35,000. But as Trotsky had predicted, even if the majority of the soldiers were not actively siding with the Bolsheviks, they weren't prepared to fight them either.

Few people in Petrograd on 25 October realized anything significant was happening until it was all over. The banks and shops were open all day, the trams were running. All the factories were open as usual – the workers had no clue Lenin was about to liberate them from capitalist exploitation. That evening the bass singing sensation Feodor Chaliapin was appearing in *Don Carlos* before a full house at the Narodny Dom* and Alexei Tolstoy's *The Death of Ivan the Terrible* was playing at the Alexandrinsky Theatre. Nightclubs and concert halls were open. Prostitutes were touting for business in the side streets around the Nevsky Prospekt as on any normal Wednesday evening. The restaurants were packed. The American journalist John

---

* A huge auditorium for cultural events of all kinds.

Reed and his wife Louise Bryant were with another group of US and British reporters dining at the Hotel de France, close to Palace Square. They returned to watch the Revolution after the *entrée*. In Soviet mythology for decades to come the Revolution was portrayed as a popular rising of the masses. Nothing could be further from the truth. Contemporary photographs show a few isolated spots around the city where a handful of Red Guards were milling about casually. There were no big crowds anywhere, no barricades, no street fighting. It is impossible to know how many people took part in the few isolated parts of the city which mattered during the insurrection. Trotsky estimated 'no more' than 25,000 but he meant that as the number of Red Guards he could have called out. The real number was far fewer – probably 10,000 at most, in a city numbering nearly 2 million.

—★—

THE TIMING OF the insurrection was crucial to the Bolsheviks' political strategy which accompanied the military takeover. The plan was to overthrow the government in order to hand 'all power to the soviets'. Of course, real power would lie with the Bolsheviks, but keeping the soviets on board gave Lenin political cover of a sort and a semblance of popular support. But there was a big snag. The all-Russia Congress of Soviets was due to meet that day, the 25th, in the splendid, white and gold ballroom of the Smolny, just below the warren of meeting places where the Bolsheviks had been planning the putsch. Lenin was supposed to present the takeover as a *fait accompli* when the Soviet Congress convened at noon and declare a 'victory' for the Revolution. However, the government still survived and the Winter Palace – symbol of power in Russia since the time of Catherine the

October: Sergey Chekhonin's cover design for an album of photomontages covering the early years of Soviet power (1921).

Great – had not fallen. Lenin had been told by his military committee that seizing the Palace would be a straightforward matter and be over within five or six hours. But it would take more than fifteen hours amid a catalogue of errors and farce.

At 9 a.m. Lenin demanded the surrender of the government. He received no reply. Prime Minister Kerensky had left soon after dawn for the army headquarters in an attempt to raise some loyal troops to defeat the rebellion.

When the ministers met in the Malachite Room in the Winter Palace towards midday they refused to surrender and decided to hold out for as long as they could. Lenin put off his appearance at the Congress of Soviets from midday to 3 p.m., but if he had to delay much further, his entire strategy might fall apart. The Palace, which had been the Provisional Government's home since July, was a vast symbol of Imperial Russia, Much of Tsarist imperial history had been played out among its 1,500 rooms, spread out over a quarter-mile- long building fronting the Neva. Along with a Company of Cossacks, there were about 220 officer cadets from the Oranienbaum mlitary school, forty members of the Petrograd Garrison's bicycle squad and 200 women from the Shock Battalion of Death. From armed forces numbering as many as 9 million Russians, this was all the Provisional Government could muster to protect the capital – and themselves.

There was no 'storming' of the Winter Palace – supposedly the centrepiece of the Revolution – as depicted in Eisenstein's epic, cinematically brilliant but largely fictional 1928 film *October*. Many more people were employed as extras for the movie than took part in the real event. Militarily it was so sloppy that Reed and Bryant strolled into the building during the afternoon without hindrance. Palace servants in their Tsarist blue uniforms took their coats and some of the cadets from the military school showed them around.

At 3 p.m. Lenin could delay no longer. He appeared before the Soviet Congress at the Smolny and brazenly declared a victory, though the government had not yet fallen, the ministers were not arrested nor the Winter Palace in Bolshevik hands. This was the first big lie of the Soviet regime. Declaring that the Bolsheviks had taken power was so important to his plan that he was prepared to invent it.

The clockwork timekeeping of the coup slipped further and further and, as the day went on, there ceased to be any deadlines at all. The Bolsheviks attempted to fire on the Palace from the Peter and Paul but the five heavy field-guns at the Fortress were museum pieces which hadn't been fired in years. Some lighter training guns were found and dragged into position, but no one could find the right three-inch shells for them. Then it turned out that the guns did not have sights. In the late afternoon the commissars worked out that the original guns simply needed cleaning.

The insurgents couldn't raise the red lantern on the top of the Fortress flagpole – the signal for the bombardment and a ground assault to begin. No red lantern could be found so the rebels abandoned any idea of giving a signal. At 6.30 p.m. the Bolsheviks, who for the last two days had control through mutinous sailors of the battle cruisers *Aurora* and *Amur*, ordered the two ships to steam upriver and halt opposite the Winter Palace. Ten minutes later they sent an ultimatum: 'Government and troops must capitulate. This ultimatum expires at 7.10 p.m. after which we will immediately open fire.'

The ministers rejected the ultimatum. At 6.50 they sat down to dinner – borscht, steamed fish and artichokes. By this point the defenders were ready to give up and bow to the inevitable. Most peeled off as the evening wore on. The Cossacks, the only ones with any military training, left 'disgusted by the Jews and wenches inside'. Fewer than 200 remained. The Red Guards could have walked in easily at any time.

At 9.40, at last, the signal was given to begin the bombardment with a blank shot fired from the *Aurora*. Twenty minutes later the guns from the Peter and Paul Fortress began firing live ammunition. A barrage of three dozen were fired but only two hit the Palace, chipping some cornices. A small group of sailors and Red Guards entered the building and quickly realized when they began to search through the rooms that they faced almost no opposition. At around 2 a.m. a little man with long wavy red hair, wearing a wide-brimmed hat and a floppy red tie bounded into the room – 'an armed mob was behind him,' according to John Reed. This colourful-looking man declared in a high-pitched voice: 'I am Vladimir Antonov-Ovseyenko, a representative of the Military Revolutionary Committee. I inform,

Red Guards outside the Smolny Institute, the Bolsheviks' headquarters, which had once been a finishing school for aristocratic girls.

all you members of the Provisional Government, that you are under arrest.' They were marched to the Peter and Paul Fortress.

In Petrograd throughout the day the casualty count was half a dozen dead, and fewer than twenty injured, all whom were caught in crossfire. The Military Committee's problem now was controlling their own Bolshevik troops. Room after room in the Palace was filled with packing cases containing some of the former Tsar's treasures, which were about to be despatched to Moscow for safekeeping. The Red Guards had different ideas. 'One man went strutting around with a bronze clock perched on his shoulder,' said Reed, who accompanied them. 'Another found a plume of ostrich feathers, which he stuck on his hat. The looting was just beginning when someone cried "Comrades! Don't take anything! This is the property of the People! Stop. Put everything back!"' Many hands dragged the spoilers down. Damask and tapestry were snatched from the arms of those who had them; two men took away the bronze clock. Roughly and hastily the things were crammed back into the cases. Other Red Guards headed straight for the Tsar's wine cellar, one of the finest in the world. It contained cases of Tokays from the age of Catherine the Great and Chateau d'Yquem 1847, Nicholas II's favourite. 'The matter of the wine [...] became critical,' recalled Antonov. 'We sent guards from picked units. They got drunk, We posted guards from Regimental Committees. They succumbed as well. A violent bacchanalia followed.' He called the Petrograd fire brigade to flood the cellar with water 'but the firemen [...] got drunk instead'.

— ★ —

THE REAL DRAMA was happening at the Smolny. That was where the Revolution was won. The Congress of Soviets convened again at

October Night by Rudolf Frentz, an artist who became a Bolshevik apparatchik after the Revolution as director of Agitprop (agitational propaganda) at the People's Commissariat of Enlightenment.

A room in the Winter Palace, whose wall was pierced by a shot from the revolutionary cruiser *Aurora* during the October 1917 Revolution.

10.30 p.m. and there was seething anger in the smoke-filled ballroom. Lenin's hope was that the coup would be rubber-stamped, but it was denounced by many delegates. Even a few Bolsheviks objected. But Lenin's opponents played right into his hands. The other socialist groups, led by Martov, said they would have 'nothing to do with this criminal takeover' and walked out of the Soviet, never to return to any position of influence in Russia. They might have made Lenin's position difficult if they had remained a strong opposition force united against the Bolsheviks. They might even have prevented Lenin from building his dictatorship. Walking out of the chamber was a fatal mistake, as many admitted soon afterwards. 'We made the Bolsheviks masters of the situation,' said Sukhanov, an opponent of Lenin. 'By leaving the Congress we gave them a monopoly on the soviets. Our own irrational decisions ensured Lenin's victory.'

At around 5 a.m., with the opposition about to stage their walkout into oblivion, the Bolsheviks most spellbinding orator, Trotsky, made one of the most famous speeches of the twentieth century, for its conclusion. The uprising 'needs no justification', he said.

> What has happened is an insurrection, not a conspiracy [...] The masses of the people followed our banner. But what do they [pointing at the other Socialists] offer us? We are told: renounce your victory, make concessions, compromise. With whom? I ask. To those who have left us we must say: you are miserable bankrupts, your role is played out. Go where you ought to go – into the dustbin of history.

Lenin said soon after 'glorious October' that taking power had been a simple thing 'as easy as picking up a feather'.

10 THE NEW WORLD

10

THE NEW WORLD

JUST BEFORE DAWN ON THE DAY OF THE REVOLUTION, WHILE the outcome still seemed uncertain, the comrades began discussing the form of the new government. Lenin wondered what it should be called. 'We must not call the members ministers,' he said. 'It's a repulsive, hackneyed word.' 'Why not Commissars,' Trotsky suggested, 'only there are too many commissars already. How about People's Commissars?' 'People's Commissars. I like that. And what shall we call the government?' 'The Council (Soviet) of People's Commissars [Sovnarkom].' 'That's wonderful,' exclaimed Lenin. 'It has the smell of revolution.'

There followed a charade of modesty among the revolutionaries.

Lenin proposed that Trotsky should be head of the government, while he himself remained leader of the Bolshevik Party. Nobody knows whether he meant it or not but he showed little surprise when Trotsky refused. 'You know very well that a Jew can't be Premier in Russia,' he said. 'And besides you'd constantly be disagreeing with me. You're the leader. It has to be you.' The decision was unanimous. Then Lenin said something perplexing given that he had spent twenty-five years of his life reading, studying, preparing for this moment. 'First we take power,' he told Trotsky, 'then we decide what to do with it.'

From the first moment, Sovnarkom felt insecure. The early Bolsheviks thought power could slip away at any time, which explains so much of the seventy-four-year history of the Soviet state. Having achieved power illegitimately, their only real concern was keeping it – an obsession they passed down to their successors. Throughout its existence the Soviet Union identified itself with the founder of the state, dead or alive. The regime Lenin created was largely shaped by his personality: secretive, conspiratorial, suspicious, intolerant, ascetic, intemperate. He wanted power for its own sake, as egotists do. But he genuinely believed that he was going to use it to improve the lives of the majority of people. It is how he justified the lies and deceit and terror that followed: everything was acceptable in pursuit of the socialist dream. As Angelica Balabonova, a longstanding Bolshevik activist and later, for a short while head of the Comintern (the Communist International organization) – who respected and admired him but grew to fear and loathe him – put it, 'It can be said of Lenin, in Goethe's phrase, "that he desired the good [...] and created evil" – and that was his great tragedy.'

Lenin wasn't interested in the trappings of power – luxury, money or sex. He always lived in very modest bourgeois style even after 1917. He didn't enjoy violence personally, unlike some of the other early Bolsheviks – yet he was responsible for the deaths of millions. He was not a sadist. He never wore anything resembling a military uniform as so many dictators favoured. He was usually in a shabby suit and tie. He knew the Bolsheviks would use terror and accepted it, always justifying it as necessary. But he never witnessed an execution and had no interest in hearing about one. To Lenin, the blood he would spill was largely theoretical.

— ★ —

NOBODY IN PETROGRAD believed the Bolsheviks would survive for long. It was a 'government of journalists and pamphleteers', who had no idea how to run an administration, according to one liberal journalist and pamphleteer. One headline on the morning after the coup described the Bolsheviks as 'Caliphs for an hour.' The leading Menshevik Irakli Tsereteli gave them 'no more than three days'. Gorky wrote in *Novaya Zhizn* that Lenin would last two weeks at the most, though he soon revised that opinion. Vladimir Nabokov, out of a job when the government was overthrown, 'refused to believe for one minute in the strength of the Bolshevik regime [...] expect its early demise'. Zinaida Gippius said, 'This government by a bunch of swindlers can't last long.' Some foreign embassies were rashly telling their governments the same. An aide to the British Ambassador cabled

The first Sovnarkom meeting, October 1917. Of the twenty-four comrades pictured here, sixteen were later either murdered in Stalin's purges or interned in the Gulag.

the Foreign Office within a few days that 'it can be taken for granted that the Bolshevik government is already on its last legs'. The American Ambassador, having told the State Department that a Bolshevik coup would never happen, now called the takeover 'a disgusting thing' and assured Washington that the Bolsheviks would soon be ousted.

Some of the senior Bolsheviks felt no more confident. One said they lived 'sitting on suitcases', so they could flee at any moment. Anatoly Lunacharsky wrote to his wife just four days after his appointment as Commissar for Enlightenment, 'Things are so unstable. Every time I break off from a letter I don't know if it will be my last. I could at any moment be thrown into jail.' The ever-practical Yakov Sverdlov, one of Lenin's most trusted lieutenants, had laid his hands on around 100,000 gold roubles, some jewels, and seven false passports – including one for himself, Lenin and other leading Bolsheviks – which he had placed in a fireproof safe in case they were forced to make a quick getaway. Nadezhda Krupskaya told comrades that Lenin's fear was that 'power may slip away from his fingers [...] and for that reason was determined not to be too lenient'.

That explained one of his first actions as chairman of Sovnarkom, on the afternoon following the coup. Having been up for two nights, Lenin slept for the morning. In his few hours' absence Kamenev had been in charge, as temporary Sovnarkom chairman. He had decreed an end to capital punishment for troops at the front, which the Kerensky government had reintroduced in the summer. Lenin's reaction was predictable. He sought out Kamenev and raged at him. 'Nonsense. How stupid. This would be a serious mistake, an unpardonable weakness. How can you make a revolution without firing squads? If you believe that we can win without executions [...] to get our way, you are under a naïve delusion. What other means of repression do we have? You don't understand the serious difficulties we are going to encounter.' From the first moment the Bolsheviks knew they would be creating their new world at the point of a gun.

For decades Soviet historians and propagandists claimed that many of the problems facing the new state could not be anticipated and from the first day the regime – supported on the whole by the masses of workers and soldiers – faced a series of emergencies. There is something to this argument, as even many foreign observers and witnesses who were not Communist sympathizers acknowledged. But detractors from the start recognized the true nature of these 'special circumstances': principally that the Bolsheviks were always a minority and felt they had to resort to repression to stay in control. The one truth that both sides accepted was that they were living in a violent age, a time of bitter warfare; brutality was commonplace in the world around 1917–19. Besides, Russia had never acquired a political culture of any collaborative politics. The Bolsheviks faced a ruined economy, inherited from the Tsars a system that for long had been accustomed to arbitrary procedures and dictatorial methods. Even if they had wanted to establish a democracy – and that seemed from the views of most of the leadership unlikely – they would have faced immense difficulties and powerful opposition. But they never took that option.

When Kerensky fled before dawn on the morning of the coup he headed straight to the front to raise an army to recapture the capital. But there was to be no return in triumph. Most of the army refused to support him – even very few of the officer corps, however much they despised the Bolsheviks. All Kerensky could muster were some four hundred Cossacks, who managed briefly to capture Gatchina, forty-five kilometres south of Petrograd. But their effort to turn the town into a strategic base from which they could seize the city fizzled out and Kerensky escaped to exile in the West. It is hard to pinpoint an exact date when the Russian Civil War began, but as good a time as any would be the departure from the scene of Alexander Kerensky and the Provisional Government.

—★—

ON DAY TWO of the Revolution the Bolsheviks began to censor the press. As the Romanovs had done, so would the Bolsheviks. A few weeks earlier, on 15 September, in one of the Party papers *Rabochi Put* (Workers' Path), Lenin had called censorship 'feudal [...] Asiatic' and praised a free press 'as much more democratic in principle than any alternative'. He promised 'incomparably more press freedom' if the Bolsheviks had their way. On 27 October Lenin wrote a Decree on the Press which established a system of censorship run by his Party apparatchiks. 'Any organ of the press may be [closed down] for inciting resistance to the Decrees of Sovnarkom [...] or if found to be sowing confusion by means of obviously defamatory distortion of the facts.' The measures were supposed to be 'temporary' against 'clear counterrevolutionaries... emergency measures must be taken to stop the torrent of filth and slander against the new authority. As soon as the new order has been firmly established all administrative measures affecting the press will be lifted and the press will be granted full freedom.' That did not happen for decades in Russia, and never entirely under the Communists. Or indeed 100 years later.

From 28 October Kadet papers were closed down. Red Guards smashed some of their presses and linotype machines and confiscated the others. A few editors and prominent journalists were arrested. The opposition press was driven underground.

The Old Left was shattered. The venerable father of Russian Marxism, Georgi Plekhanov, now sixty-one and in poor health, was horrified that his erstwhile comrade had taken power for himself and his Party, sidelining other socialists. The day after the coup he wrote an Open Letter to the Petrograd Working Class saying the Bolshevik 'revolution is the greatest historic calamity, which will turn back the clock from all the gains made in Russia since February'. The next day soldiers and sailors burst into his Petrograd apartment and drew a pistol on him, though they left him unharmed. A week after the Revolution, Vera Zasulich, sixty-eight, who had spent long years in exile with Lenin and Trotsky, told a comrade in despair: 'I feel as though everything I struggled for, everything that was so dear to me my entire life has crumbled to dust.'

To much of the European Left at the time, the Bolsheviks were not socialists at all. Their view of the 'dictatorship of the proletariat', of class-based discrimination, of imposing an ideology through terror, was not what most of them believed. Lenin was at the very far edge, the outer reaches, of socialist thought. After October, many socialists elsewhere foresaw, as did the redoubtable Rosa Luxemburg, that his regime would result in permanent dictatorship, growing ever harsher. They loathed Bolshevik principles. But they resented even more the effect they would have on them and their own domestic politics. The Revolution brought them and their ideas into disrepute at home. It was irrelevant that the more moderate socialists hated the Bolsheviks. It was easy in right-wing propaganda to show that all socialists were all the same – as would happen throughout the rest of the twentieth century.

—★—

For the first weeks after the Revolution the Bolsheviks ruled by decree. Dozens of them came from the Smolny in a flurry – most written by Lenin himself. Apart from the Decree on the Press, there were decrees on Peace, which promised a swift end to the war; on Land, which

We Are Victorious, by an unknown artist, was the most widely circulated poster
produced by the Bolshevik regime in the year that followed the October Revolution.

promised a vast agrarian reform that gave peasants rights to own and control estates; and on Workers' Rights, which assured 'freedom from capitalist exploitation' and control over factories. A decree guaranteed an eight-hour working day – something for which the trade unions had been struggling for decades. All the nations of the Russian empire, from Armenia to the Baltic states and Poland, were given the right to independence. Women were ensured equal rights in work, marriage and over family property. Russians were assured freedom of religion – and of none. Under the old regime the Orthodox Church was the established religion, many others had been banned and there were still ecclesiastical courts which had considerable power. Decrees nationalized the banks and major industries. The name of the Russian Social Democratic Workers' Party, which had existed since the 1890s, was changed to Communist Party (Bolshevik) within a month of the October Revolution. It was a signal: the Party was on the path from socialism to Communism.

The frenetic pace of the decrees was partly due to the Bolsheviks' determination to move forward with speed. But the main reason was prompted by insecurity: if the regime didn't survive they wanted the evidence of the decrees to remind history of the things they intended the Revolution to achieve. The decrees were agreed by Sovnarkom, but hardly even discussed by the soviets in whose name the Bolsheviks had taken power. Quickly the Soviet became the rubber-stamp body it would remain for the next seven decades – 'a sorry parody of a revolutionary parliament,' as Adolph Joffe, one of Trotsky's best friends, remarked.

—★—

A SECRET DECREE written by Lenin established the Cheka, the main building block for the Soviet police state. There were numerous name changes over the years – the GPU, GPRU, NKVD, MGB and finally, in its best-known incarnation, the KGB. Whatever it was called, its tasks remained the same: to protect the Party and its leadership from any perceived threat of subversion, and to dispense 'revolutionary justice'. It was the Communist Party's 'sword and shield'. Most operatives called themselves Chekists, up to the day it was disbanded in the 1990s. The Russian president a hundred years after the Revolution, Vladimir Putin, a long-serving KGB officer until

Felix Dzerzhinsky, the 'Red Count', photographed in 1918. As first head of the Soviet secret police organisation known as the Cheka, he was Lenin's willing executioner and architect of the 'Red Terror' (1918–22).

the collapse of the USSR, used to say he had been a Chekist. So did thousands of people who worked for the imitation agencies the Cheka spawned throughout the Communist world – the East German Stasi or the *Securitate* in Nicolae Ceauşescu's Romania.

It was set up six weeks after the Revolution as the Extraordinary Commission (Chrezhvychniaia Komissia) for Combating Counter-Revolution, Speculation and Sabotage. Officially the Cheka was supposed to work hand in hand with a separate Commission established three days earlier to combat 'wine pogroms' by people looting the cellars of the Tsar and the rich. But the Cheka's remit was always intended to be wider, though its functions and powers were not made public until the mid-1920s. From the first it operated outside the law under top secret protocols with virtually no political accountability.

The Soviet had no control and neither, over the years, did Sovnarkom. At first it answered only to Lenin, then to Stalin and later to whoever emerged as the General Secretary of the Party. Soon the Cheka became the most feared of the state 'organs', and its first chief, the 'ruthless, cold, shy and deeply puritanical'* Felix Dzerzhinsky, a Polish count, the most hated man in Russia. Dzerzhinsky was clear about his task, 'To fight a merciless war against all enemies of the Revolution. We don't look for forms of justice. We are not in need of justice. It is war now – face to face, a fight to the finish. Life or death.' The Cheka was more ruthless than the Okhrana, but it is a question of degree and not a category difference. In many ways they were mirror images of each other. The Okhrana had operated as a private police force of the Crown – the Tsar's sword and shield. The Cheka's role was similar and so were its techniques.

— ★ —

THE WAR HAD triggered the Revolution – both revolutions – and the Bolsheviks knew they had to deliver on the promise of peace if they were to avoid the fate of the Provisional Government. Lenin was prepared to make peace at almost any price, though there was a large group in the Party against him and he had to work hard to muster a majority in support. It was an article of faith among the Bolsheviks that Revolution in Russia would spark immediate uprisings in Western Europe and advance world Revolution. With each small-scale army mutiny in Germany, Britain or France the Bolshevik press anticipated an insurrection among workers that would bring down the bourgeois government. For much of the new regime's leadership a peace deal was more a practical issue than one of socialist theory. Lenin believed

* Sukhanov, *The Russian Revolution 1917: A Personal Record.*

his Revolution could not survive on its own for long amid a sea of enemies, so the Bolsheviks urgently needed time to consolidate without foreign wars – and wait for the other revolutions to follow, with some encouragement (and later financial help). 'I am prepared to yield territory to [the Germans] to obtain a breathing space,' he told comrades a few days after the coup in October. 'For us, as well as for the international point of view, the preservation of the Soviet republic stands above all else.'

The peace deal with Germany was the first big test of the Bolsheviks' power in the new Russia – and they nearly failed. It opened a split within the Party that might have toppled the regime within a few weeks. At first most of the comrades refused to approve an abject deal negotiated with the Germans that gave the Central Powers everything they had wanted. The Treaty of Brest-Litovsk was, as Lenin's wife said, 'enslavement, partition, humiliation' but probably ensured the survival of the fledgling Soviet state. Apart from the territory they had already lost over the previous three years in Byelorussia and the Ukrainian borderlands, they lost almost the whole of the rest of Ukraine, Finland and the Baltic states to Germany, and three ports on the Black Sea to the Turks – 1.8 million square kilometres, 62 million people, around 30 per cent of its best agricultural land and half its industry and coalmines. Already facing an economic disaster with inflation and food shortages they had to pay a huge indemnity to Germany of around 120 million gold roubles, more than a quarter of the state's reserves.

That no successful socialist revolutions did follow was a blow in practical and ideological terms that damaged the Left's standing and influence. The price of peace was immense and not only in land, gold and reputational damage. Russia's separate peace with Germany caused the first major collision between the Western powers and the new socialist state – the original Cold War with the Soviets.

11

DICTATORSHIP OVER THE PROLETARIAT

11

DICTATORSHIP OVER THE PROLETARIAT

Russia's first freely elected parliament – the Constituent Assembly – survived for about twelve hours. There would not be another for nearly seventy-five years.

The introduction of a representative democracy was the single biggest promise the Provisional Government made after the Tsar was overthrown. Originally the date for the elections was set for September; then it was pushed back to October and finally to mid-November. Polling would be staggered over two weeks because of the size of the country and the huge logistical task of counting the votes.

Each time the elections were postponed the Bolsheviks complained that the government intended to 'strangle democracy' and was planning to cheat people of the 'free parliament they have struggled for'. But the Bolsheviks under Lenin had no intention of allowing a free parliament. For tactical reasons their propagandists on occasions in the past wrote in praise of elections. But they – in particular Lenin – didn't believe in 'bourgeois democracy' on principle and certainly not in practice for a revolutionary state. The dictatorship of the proletariat and the authority of the Soviet were 'not only a higher form of democracy [but] the only form of democracy'.

On the first day after the coup, within hours of seizing power, Lenin had wanted to postpone the elections indefinitely. 'We have to put them off,' he told his circle of comrades. 'They may cost the Revolution its head.' But reluctantly he was persuaded by his closest lieutenant at that time, Yakov Sverdlov and most of his entourage, to let them go ahead as planned.

Immediately he regretted it. Lenin knew the Bolsheviks would not perform well. But they did even worse than he expected and won fewer than 10 million votes, around 22 per cent of the total, which made a nonsense of the claim that they were supported by the masses. Almost all their vote came from the working class in Petrograd, Moscow and some other cities with an industrial base and a large population of ethnic Russians. The Socialist Revolutionaries (SRs) won by far the most votes – 39 per cent of the total, though their success was complicated because they split into two before the campaign began. It was seldom clear to voters whether a candidate was a 'Right' SR, which was opposed to the Bolsheviks, or a 'Left' SR, which was friendlier to them and at the beginning of December 1917 became the only coalition partner allied to Lenin's Party. The Mensheviks got only 3 per cent of the vote and the Kadets 5 per cent. Historians who have since argued that the Russians in 1917 showed themselves to be moderate reformers were way off the mark. The vast majority of the votes – around 85 per cent – went to Leftist revolutionaries of one type or another, though clearly people had not voted for a one-party state under the Bolsheviks.

The Bolsheviks delayed the opening of the Assembly, while plotting ways of abolishing it altogether. First the politically neutral Electoral Commissioners, whose job was to oversee practical arrangements for running the election, was fired and replaced by a Bolshevik Party apparatchik.

On 27 November, the right-of-centre Kadet Party was banned and its members declared 'enemies of the people'; Red Guards arrested every prominent Kadet they could find – dozens of people, many of whom had just been elected to the Assembly.

When Lenin could put off the day no longer, on 5 January the Assembly gathered at the Tauride Palace. Petrograd was 'in a state of siege' from early in the morning. The government had declared martial law and flooded the city with loyal troops and Red Guards. Demonstrations had been banned, but at noon around 40,000 workers, students and civil servants defied the order and began to march the mile and a half or so from the Field of Mars to the Tauride Palace, on a bitterly cold and snowy day. When they reached the Liteyny Prospekt, Red Guards, hidden from rooftops, opened fire. The protestors scattered and two huge banners they had been carrying –

Yakov Sverdlov, Lenin's second-in-command. Until his death in 1919 in the post-war flu pandemic, Sverdlov looked the most likely man to succeed as leader of the regime.

'All Power to the Assembly' – lay trampled in the slush. At least ten people were killed and seventy seriously wounded.

When the chamber filled and proceedings began in the afternoon there were armed guards scattered throughout the hall and several of the deputies now had weapons with them too. Carl Lindhagen, the Mayor of Stockholm who had met Lenin nine months earlier during the 'sealed train' journey, and was now in Petrograd as an observer, commented: 'It's going to be a Wild West show today [...] everyone's carrying a gun.' This was not how things were done in Sweden.

The SR leader Viktor Chernov was elected to the Assembly chair and made a long rambling speech denouncing the Revolution. The Bolsheviks, vastly outnumbered, jeered him throughout. After he had finished, the serious business began. Sverdlov proposed a Bolshevik motion calling on the Assembly automatically to ratify Sovnarkom decrees as a rubber-stamp body – beginning with the Decree on the Rights of Workers and including the nationalization of the banks, and a Decree on compulsory labour 'to destroy the bourgeois class of parasites'.

It was defeated by a big margin and the Bolsheviks walked out – 'We won't stay in this counterrevolutionary body,' said the leader of the Kronstadt sailors, Fyodor Raskolnikov. There was an adjournment and Lenin then gave the order to dissolve the Assembly. He ordered the Red Guards not to use violence, but told them that when the deputies left later that night the Palace should be locked up and nobody was to be allowed back in the next day.

When delegates filled the chamber again at around 11.30 p.m. the speeches became longer and duller. At around 4 a.m. the War Minister Pavel Dybenko ordered Red Guards to empty the chamber. One of the guards approached Chernov on the podium, tapped him on the shoulder and said, 'Everybody here should leave the chamber now because the guards are tired.' Chernov told him that, 'We are also tired but that cannot interrupt our work which all Russia is watching.' The guards, most of whom were drunk, began fingering their weapons menacingly and turning the lights off one by one. At 4.40 a.m. on 6 January all the delegates filed out and the gates of the Palace were locked behind them. When they began to return to the Tauride the next afternoon the way was barred by soldiers and a decree was posted on the Palace gates dissolving the Assembly. So much for representative democracy.

—★—

A WAVE OF CRIME and anarchy spreading through Petrograd and other major cities was a dilemma for the Bolsheviks. Random violence and thefts had been a growing problem since the February Revolution and now that the Bolsheviks were the power in Russia they were expected to deal with the problem. On the other hand Bolshevik agitators – Vladimir Lenin chief among them – was himself encouraging much of the violence for political reasons – as people's revenge against the bourgeoisie for 'centuries of gross inequality' and as 'revolutionary justice against the exploiters'. At first his rhetoric had considerable appeal: wasn't this what the Revolution was all about, to abolish privilege? The 'settling of accounts with the bourgeoisie', in Dzerzhinsky's favourite phrase, began before the Cheka took control of the terror.

The apartments of the rich were robbed and vandalized, they were attacked on the streets, they were routinely abused. People took revenge into their own hands – and Bolshevik agitprop egged them on. In mid-December a Sovnarkom decree declared that those who 'hoarded' food or wealth were 'enemies of the people' and called for:

> a war to the death against the rich, the idlers and parasites, [citizens must] cleanse the Russian land of all vermin, of scoundrel fleas, the bedbug rich [...] in one place they can jail a dozen rich men, a dozen scoundrels, half a dozen workers who shirk on the job [...] in another place they will be out to work on cleaning latrines.

The rich and privileged were branded 'former people', awarded far lower rations, and were placed at the back of the queues for bread. Some scions of great aristocratic families starved to death. Middle-class families were made to share their homes with the poor and often ended up with the smaller rooms in a larger apartment – a revolution in domestic life, a new world, where the servants and masters literally changed places. The revenge notion was justified by Trotsky in a robust, if chilling, way: 'For centuries our fathers and grandfathers have been cleaning up the dirt and filth of the ruling classes, but now we will make them clean up our dirt. We must make life so uncomfortable for them that they will lose the desire to remain bourgeois.' Or, often, they lost the will to stay in Russia at all in a New World that was clearly not meant for them – as the Constitution of the Republic proclaimed in July 1918. The State was described officially on a Sovnarkom decree as 'a dictatorship of the urban and rural proletariat and the poorest'. Those who had employed more than one other person were denied voting rights. Many of the 'former people' went into hiding in an attempt to hold out until the chaos was over or the Bolsheviks overthrown or emigrated. They took boats across the Black Sea, trains to Finland and, if they could, to Poland. Panic set in among the bourgeoisie. Around 3 million people left the country in the first two and a half years after the October Revolution.

One decree codified Bolshevik ideas of 'revolutionary justice'. At a stroke, the existing legal system was abolished. Though it kept the Tsarist principle that there was one system of justice for normal crimes against property and the person, and separate laws for crimes against the state. 'People's Courts' were for common criminals – essentially ad hoc mob trials in which twelve 'elected' judges, many of them barely literate, would rule less on the facts of a case than with the use of 'revolutionary conscience'. Court proceedings were not evidence based, the procedures were more or less made up as they went along. There were cases of some people being convicted on the basis of 'denunciations' by neighbours, those involved in long-term family feuds, and women denouncing their unfaithful husbands.

Another new judicial creation was borrowed from the French Revolution – the Revolutionary Tribunals. They dealt with crimes against the state and were popular for a year or so but were phased out over time. Public trials were replaced by closed ten-minute hearings by a 'troika' of Party members operated by the Cheka. In the Communist Party newspaper *Pravda*, Lenin explained the theory behind the concept of revolutionary justice:

> For us there do not, and cannot, exist the old system of morality and 'humanity' invented by the bourgeoisie for the purpose of oppressing and exploiting the 'lower classes'. Our morality is new, our humanity is absolute, for it rests on the ideal of destroying all oppression and coercion. To us, all is permitted, for we are the first in the world to raise the sword not in the name of enslaving or oppressing anyone, but in the name of freeing all from bondage [...] Blood? Let there be blood, if it alone can turn the grey-white-and-black banner of the old piratical world to a scarlet hue, for only the complete and final death of that old world will save us from the return of the old jackals.

On 21 February 1918* Lenin issued a decree – 'The Socialist Fatherland in Danger' – written in his familiar literary style – which allowed Red Guards to 'shoot on the spot [...] enemy agents, profiteers, marauders, hooligans and counterrevolutionary agitators'.

---

* This date, and all dates from here on, follow the Gregorian (Western) calendar. Russia adopted the Gregorian calendar in February 1918.

The Justice Commissar Isaac Steinberg protested and told Lenin that such harsh measures would 'destroy the revolution'. Lenin replied: 'On the contrary [...] do you really believe that we can be victorious without the very cruellest revolutionary terror?'

'Then why do we bother with a Commissariat of Justice at all?' Steinberg replied. 'Let's call it frankly The Commissariat for Social Extermination and be done with it.' Lenin's face lit up, according to Steinberg, and he said 'Well put. That's exactly what it should be; but we can't say that.'

—★—

MUCH OF RUSSIA was hungry – and the Bolsheviks had to find someone to blame. From the first they scapegoated the farmers. The Bolsheviks didn't create the food crisis; the dislocation of the war, a transport system that had completely broken down and two successive poor harvests were all major causes. But the new regime's punitive policies of compulsion and terror in the countryside made things worse.

The Bolsheviks needed an enemy. So they invented a new class of Russian – kulaks, or rich peasants – who they claimed were hoarding grain and deliberately starving the rest of the country, particularly the cities. The word kulak means, literally, fist (and refers to 'tight-fisted' people). In reality there were very few rich peasants in Russia – a small number owned any substantial amount of land, some were money lenders to other peasants, a few possessed more than one horse, cow or a plough. Fewer than 2 per cent of peasant households employed anybody outside their own family. The campaign against kulaks was an extension of the class war being waged in the cities. Rigorous Marxists always suspected rural life and the peasantry – a 'backward class', still semi-feudal, which

Тов. Ленин ОЧИЩАЕТ
землю от нечисти.

Viktor Deni's poster *Comrade Lenin Cleans Up the World*. From 1919, images of the Soviet leader were ubiquitous in Russia – the first signs of the phenomenon of the 'personality cult' that would disfigure so many Communist regimes.

stood in the way of historical development towards socialism, according to the German oracle himself. Most of the Bolsheviks were from the urban intelligentsia, which generally despised the *muzhiks* for being part of superstitious, illiterate Old Russia. The Bolsheviks suspected – perhaps rightly – that the peasantry would never support them, unless they were coerced and bullied into obedience. Before the Revolution the Bolsheviks promised that the peasants would be given land seized from the big landowners – the nobles, big industrialists and the Church. There was little talk of that after the coup.

Food shortages worsened during 1918 and hit the cities hardest – partly because the transport system was so poor that distribution was a huge problem, and partly because of inflation. Money was worthless following the Revolution and farmers refused to be paid in cash. The mint which had employed around 3,000 people in 1917 had a staff of 13,500 a year later – 'Printing money was the only growth industry,' said Sukhanov, not entirely in jest. Within a year the number of roubles in circulation rose from 60 billion to 225 billion. An entire parallel system of payment in kind and barter was created. Some strict Bolsheviks, experimenting with supposedly socialist economic theories, thought inflation a good thing because it would destroy the reliance of the economy on money. Lenin disagreed and realized what it would do to the value of everything, but like so many leaders throughout history he was powerless to deal with inflation once it had taken hold.

Millions of people were leaving the cities in the hope that there would be more food in the country, which for a while there was. Petrograd lost two-thirds of its population within eighteen months. 'Dead horses are lying in the streets; dogs eat them,' Gorky wrote to his wife. Very soon people were eating them too – in a country where, unlike in France at the time, horsemeat was by no means considered a delicacy.

Zinaida Gippius said most of her friends, the 'former people', had 'distended stomachs [...] by the spring of 1919 practically all of them had become unrecognizable'. Some of the intellectuals were 'on the books... working for the Bolsheviks as minor clerks. They are given just enough to die of hunger but slowly.'

The Bolsheviks' answer to the food crisis was increased compulsion. They launched a 'battle for grain' in early summer 1918, blaming the *kulaks* and the 'profiteers' for hunger in Russia. In a radio speech, Lenin said:

> The kulaks are the rabid foes of the people [...] these bloodsuckers have grown rich on the hunger of the people. These spiders have grown fat out of the workers. These leeches have sucked the blood of the working people and grown richer as the workers in the cities have starved. Ruthless war on the kulaks! Death to all of them.

The regime set a fixed rate the government would pay for corn and other grains at mid-1916 prices – absurd when inflation had increased at least sevenfold in the last year and a half. When peasants refused to sell at that price, hid their stock and seeds, or threatened to replant crops that weren't covered by fixed prices, the Bolsheviks used force. A Food Commissariat established a system of grain requisitions: 'using armed detachments of workers and Red Guards [...] we will conduct a merciless war.'

Requisition brigades, as they were called, were sent to more than 20,000 villages within the first two months of the decree. Usually they consisted of seventy-five men, armed with machine guns, who would surround a village and demand that peasants hand over a set yield of grain decided by the local Bolshevik Party headquarters. Any peasant who did not hand over the required amount of grain could be executed on the spot, and many were. The brigades routinely tortured suspects until the 'right' amount of grain was found. One Bolshevik official who saw a Brigade sweep through a village in the 'Black Earth' region of southern Russia was shocked. 'The measures of extraction are reminiscent of a medieval inquisition. They make the peasants strip and kneel on the ground, whip or beat them, sometimes kill them.' Lenin personally suggested an added twist on the 'class war in the villages'. He said that when punishments were inflicted, the brigades 'should call upon at least six witnesses who must be picked from the poor population of the neighbourhood'. There were cases of the brigades holding twenty or thirty villagers ransom until the amount of grain they demanded was handed over.

During the first spring and summer after seizing power Lenin continually called for tougher action. On 10 August 1918 he wrote to the Bolsheviks in Penza Province, south-east of Moscow:

> Comrades, the Kulak uprising in your five districts must be crushed without pity. The interests of the whole revolution demand it, for the final and decisive battle with the kulaks everywhere is now engaged. An example must be made. 1) Hang (and I mean hang, so the people can see) not less than 100 known kulaks, rich men, bloodsuckers. 2) Publish their names. 3) Identify hostages [...] Do this so that for hundreds of miles around the people can see, tremble, know and cry: they are killing and will go on killing the bloodsucking kulaks. Cable that you have received this and carried out (instructions). Yours, Lenin. PS Find tougher people

At least 2,700 villagers were killed, probably many more, in the first year of food requisitions. Entire villages were burned down, or the seed supply used for planting the next year's crop was confiscated leaving the peasants destitute. The 'battle for grain' was justified because it would pacify rural Russia and 'this is the meaning of the dictatorship of the proletariat', Lenin insisted. Joseph Stalin – a figure of growing importance in Sovnarkom alongside Lenin, Trotsky and Sverdlov – was posted to Tsaritsyn (later renamed Stalingrad; but then, as now, Volgograd) in June 1918 to secure food supplies. He purged the city of anyone suspected of being a counterrevolutionary. This wasn't tough enough for Lenin who ordered him to be yet more ruthless – 'be merciless,' he cabled. Stalin replied swiftly, 'Be assured our hand will not tremble.'

A young Stalin, taken around 1907 when he was organizing heists to raise money for the Bolsheviks – a practice the Marxists called 'stealing what has already been stolen'.

But the campaign was having little effect on Russia's supply of food. In the first year requisitions yielded little extra grain. Even by the government's official figures the food brigades collected only about 570,000 tons – from a total harvest yield of 49 million tons. Lenin later wound down the food brigades and his rhetoric against the peasants. He tried a different tactic to get them on his side. But campaigns against and forcing farmers at gunpoint to produce for the state became a feature of Soviet life for decades to come. The most extreme example would be the famine that Stalin deliberately brought about in Ukraine in 1932–3.

ЧТОБЫ БОЛЬШЕ ИМЕТЬ -
НАДО БОЛЬШЕ ПРОИЗВОДИТЬ

ЧТОБЫ БОЛЬШЕ
ПРОИЗВОДИТЬ -
НАДО БОЛЬШЕ
ЗНАТЬ

The Soviet regime used posters for education as well as propaganda.
Alexander Zelensky's powerful *To Know More You Must Produce More*
was displayed in thousands of factories – and schools.

CIVIL WAR: REDS AND WHITES

12

12

CIVIL WAR: REDS AND WHITES

WHILE THE COUP IN PETROGRAD HAD BEEN GENERALLY peaceful, there was fighting for nearly two weeks in Moscow between Red Guards and troops loyal to Kerensky. Around a thousand people had been killed, mostly soldiers and some civilians caught in the crossfire. When the Bolsheviks moved the Russian capital from Petrograd to Moscow on 10 March 1918 – because they were worried that, despite the peace treaty, the Germans (who had control of swathes of what had been the Russian empire) could easily march on Petrograd – rubble was lying in Red Square and many surrounding streets. Some of Moscow's finest old buildings, including St Basil's Cathedral, had been badly damaged. The stucco of several of the biggest palaces and mansions was studded with bullet holes. A counter coup by Left Revolutionaries, one-time coalition allies of the Bolsheviks, but bitter enemies since the peace deal with the Germans and the regime's brutal campaigns against the peasants, was suppressed, but not before Dzerzhinsky had been held hostage.

Serious armed opposition against the regime eventually coalesced around a group of armies known as the 'Whites'. Again Lenin was lucky in his enemy. By contrast with the Bolsheviks, who despite a few ideological splits possessed a unified leadership, the

Whites were fragmented; there were three main armies separated by thousands of miles. Even when they managed to communicate over such vast distances, their leaders often loathed each other, and had strong disagreements about strategy and tactics. There were all kinds of practical and military reasons the Whites lost the war: they controlled a smaller population to recruit from, their problems with communications were insuperable. But the main reason ran deeper. The Whites were stuck in the past – they were 'the last dream of the old world', as Marina Tsvetaeva, one of their passionate devotees, put it. Most Russians – and the minority groups in the empire, from Finland to the Caucasus – may have loathed and feared the Bolsheviks; but nor did they want a return to the past. 'We didn't put forward a single new idea,' acknowledged one of the Whites' own leaders, Vasily Shulgin, in the summer of 1919. And when after two and a half years,

Trotsky created the Red Army from the ruins of the force that was demoralized and beaten in the First World War. Here he exhorts troops during the Civil War in 1919.

millions dead from war, disease and hunger, they were defeated, most acknowledged why. 'Their old regime psychology prevented the Whites from facing the new world the revolutions had created,' Peter Struve, once a far Left socialist and friend of Lenin, who had turned into a reformist moderate, said years later.

> They conducted themselves as though nothing had happened whereas in reality the whole world around them had collapsed and in order to defeat the enemy they themselves had to undergo a rebirth [...] In the revolutionary storm that struck Russia in 1917 even out-and-out restorationists had to turn revolutionaries [...] because in a revolution only revolutionaries can find their way.

—★—

TROTSKY WAS placed in charge of the Bolsheviks' new Red Army. For orthodox Marxists the very idea of a standing army was anathema – armies had existed to oppress the working class and forestall revolution. But needs must... Trotsky realized the Bolsheviks couldn't rely on a ragbag assortment of former private soldiers, who had just been beaten in a war, and untrained factory workers like the Red Guards. They needed a proficient unit fast and the only way was to use Tsarist officers with experience to establish a force, train the other ranks at speed and then lead them. Many Bolsheviks in the existing army and Party members objected that a) 'class enemies' were being given special treatment ahead of their own people and b) the Tsarist officers would betray the regime, given half the chance. But Lenin backed Trotsky and between them they built up an efficient unit.

The Red Army was formed by the Tsarist officer corps. More than 8,000 volunteered immediately after the Revolution, including around fifty generals. They were mostly career soldiers who would serve a civilian government, whatever its politics. Many had joined up before the Brest-Litovsk Treaty was signed, when it looked as though the Germans might sweep through Russia, and they acted from patriotism. Others wanted to be on the winning side, and they bet on the Bolsheviks.

Increasing numbers of volunteers joined up when they could see the Red Army was turning into a professional outfit. Altogether more than 50,000 Tsarist officers joined the Reds in the Civil War, most of them because their families were held hostage if they didn't. They were told they would be watched by a commissar and if they did anything suspicious they would be shot and/or their families would be arrested. Only those who had relatives in Russia were recruited. Trotsky's 'Special Order No. 30' in September 1918 stated: 'Let the turncoats realize that they are at the same time betraying their own [...] fathers, mothers, sisters, brothers, wives and children.'

A ceramic plate by the artist Mikhail Adamovich, featuring the head of Lenin. Propaganda appeared everywhere – even on household crockery.

Trotsky was a harsh disciplinarian who routinely had people executed. The idea that in principle he was a more pacific and tolerant figure than Stalin is entirely inaccurate and based on his own rewriting of history after he lost power and was in exile. But he was decisive and he had a clear, logical mind. He was loathed by many Party members for his arrogance and hauteur, his perfectly pressed uniforms and his swagger. But nobody could deny his energy or his showmanship. He crisscrossed Russia in his special train equipped with a printing press, telegraph machines, an orchestra and a film crew and gave electrifying performances to rally often jaded and unwilling troops. He was the Red Army's persuader-in-chief.

— ★ —

THE WHITES HAD some competent military leaders. Anton Denikin, head of the Voluntary Army in the south, was a brilliant tactician, as was Baron Pyotr Wrangel. But they quarrelled with each other. Some wanted the monarchy back, most wanted to return the estates to the pre-1917 landlords, a few wanted a Western-style democracy. None wanted independence for the nations within the Russian empire. Technically the most senior White commander, Alexander Kolchak, based in Siberia – who styled himself grandly 'Supreme Leader of Eastern Russia and Siberia' – was pressed by various nationalist groups to give them something. He refused repeatedly, however, saying at one point, 'History would never forgive me if I gave up what Peter the Great won.' They received no real support in Ukraine, Crimea or the Caucasus. Finland and the Baltic states were neutral in the Civil War, a great boon to the Bolsheviks, who promised the nationalities anything and everything – a range of freedoms they knew that in victory they would never keep. The Whites were offering very little and increasingly they found it hard to recruit soldiers. Like the Reds, they had to conscript soldiers, used press gangs and resorted to terror.

— ★ —

THERE WAS SAVAGE barbarity on both sides during the Russian Civil War. Accurate casualty figures are impossible to come by, but probably

The Last Battle – A Call to Arms. A poster produced at a time in mid-1918 when the Reds feared they could lose the Civil War.

amounted to between 5 and 6 million dead. Neither Reds nor Whites could depend on the loyalty of the people under their control. On the whole the civilian population – mostly peasants – took a 'plague on both your houses' view. They hated the Bolshevik grain requisitions, but the Whites never accepted that there had been a revolution on the land; most of the Whites wanted to turn the clock back and restore the estates to the old landowners. Both sides forced civilians to join their armies, but the peasants didn't want to fight. Millions voted with their feet and deserted from both sides.

Bolshevik central command in Moscow deluged local Red Army commanders and Communist Party bosses with directives and telegrams designed to motivate or terrify. Lenin would fire off telegrams daily with the word 'shoot' repeated alarmingly and casually. They make the grimmest reading. In September 1918 he told the Party boss in Saratov 'temporarily to appoint your own army commanders and shoot conspirators and waverers without asking anyone or idiotic red tape'. A few days later he wrote to the leaders of the Soviet in the Caucasus, 'If there is an offensive in Baku [where there were big oil refineries] make preparations to burn Baku down *totally*.' When Kazan was besieged a month later he cabled Trotsky: 'There must be no question of taking pity on the town and putting matters off any longer [...] merciless annihilation is what is vital once it is established that Kazan is enclosed in an iron ring.' He ordered a commander that 'the taking of hostages from the bourgeoisie and from officers' families must be stepped up in view of the increased instances of treason'.

Historians have written vast amounts about the brutality of the Bolsheviks and there are plenty of examples. Often over the years the atrocities committed by the Whites have been ignored or excused. One has to wonder, though, if the Whites had won the Civil War –

one of the great counterfactual 'ifs' in history – whether the sufferings of Russia's peasants or workers would have been that much less than they turned out to be – at least in the short to medium term. The Whites were probably too disorganized and disunited to organize a totalitarian state, but a vicious tyranny of some kind would not have been beyond them. Very few of their chief personalities were decent liberals with democratic tendencies.

To supporters such as Tsvetaeva, the Whites were the 'youth and glory of Russia'. But to most Russians they seemed as savage as the Bolsheviks. The Whites, as an American observer of the war put it, 'seldom rose above anarchic warlordism'. Kerensky agreed. He said in the summer of 1919, 'There is no crime the [White armies] would not commit [...] often the population of whole villages have been flogged, including the teachers and intellectuals.'

In one village, Lezhanka, near Rostov, officers slaughtered sixty peasants in cold blood, including old men and women. Hundreds of villagers were stripped and whipped while other groups of Volunteer Army officers stood by and watched, many of them laughing. It was a routine attack; there were scores of incidents like it. 'We had not brought pardon and peace with us, but only the cruel sword of vengeance,' admitted Baron Wrangel later in exile.

As so often in Russian history, it was the Jews who were directly targeted. At one point in the summer of 1919 Denikin's Volunteer Army reached a point only 250 miles from Moscow. But that was the high point of their success. They were overstretched, could not maintain their supply lines, and when they faced a counterattack, they were forced to retreat. As the army withdrew it launched an orgy of bloody pogroms. The commander did nothing to stop them while his political officers spewed out antisemitic propaganda: all Communists were Jews, it was the Jews who murdered the Tsar. Trotsky – 'real name

Peace and Freedom in Soviet Russia – a poster produced by the Whites, depicting Trotsky as a blood-soaked monster.

Bronstein, the Jewish mass killer' – was singled out as the archcriminal. Bolshevism was blamed on Jews so it was entirely legitimate to slaughter them, the White propaganda said. Between 1–5 October 1919 the Jewish quarter of Kyiv was attacked. Soldiers demanded money, killed and raped while their officers urged them on – 'Yids are killing our people and they all support the Bolsheviks,' one officer told his men.* In Chernobyl Jews were herded into the synagogue and the building was set on fire. As they were being defeated by the Bolsheviks, the Whites slaughtered about 150,000 civilians.

There were a few pogroms by the Reds, though an almost insignificant number compared to the Volunteer Army's orchestrated savagery and Lenin removed officers if he heard even a rumour of their involvement. Lenin was many unattractive things and as we have seen felt no sentimental compunction against using violent methods; but he was not an antisemite.

—★—

THE WESTERN ALLIES bankrolled the Whites with large amounts of money and arms – and lied about it. They supported the Whites, but so half-heartedly that their intervention made no difference.

They felt entirely justified in doing *something*. The Brest-Litovsk peace had broken treaties with Britain and France. The Germans had moved regiments that were based in the East to the Western Front. The Bolsheviks had seized vast amounts of foreign assets, including those of many US companies. They were refusing to pay loans taken by the Tsarist government. They were threatening to spread

* Colonel Vasily Lupokhin, cited in Geoffrey Swain, *The Russian Civil War* (The History Press, London, 2008).

revolution everywhere, with campaigns of propaganda and subversion throughout the world. They were seen as dangerous – but the Allies could not agree on what to do about them.

Within weeks of the October Revolution the British had decided they would help the Whites. They had a few thousand troops in the ports of Archangel and Murmansk in northern Russia, who had been there since the start of the First World War to supply the Russian military. After the Bolshevik coup, they remained there for most of the Civil War, occasionally skirmishing with the Red Army, but now supplying Kolchak and Denikin. Officially they claimed they were neutral and denied they were helping the Whites, but they were fooling nobody – certainly not the Bolsheviks. The British were by far the biggest financial backers of the Whites. Altogether they gave them more than £100 million, a vast sum at the time. They also sent several spies to help mount plots to undermine the Bolshevik government.

The Americans lied too – principally to hide the truth to their own people, rather than to deceive the Russians. President Woodrow Wilson and Secretary of State Robert Lansing – a cold warrior before the term was invented – wanted to help the Whites, but secretly and semi-legally. American law forbade the government from granting loans to independent armies. Lansing devised a plan to lend money to the British and French to pass on to the Whites. A small corps of US troops went to Archangel for a few months from the summer of 1918 and 200 American soldiers died fighting the Bolsheviks.

But Wilson and British Prime Minister David Lloyd George were reluctant to commit themselves too far while there was still a war to win against Germany. And when the First World War was over, it was too late. They approved money for the Whites, and they encouraged the Czech Brigade, an army of nearly 40,000 soldiers which was supposed

Women, Take up your Rifles! – the Bolsheviks were desperately keen to recruit women into the Red Army.

to be crossing Russia eastwards on their way back to Europe, to fight the Bolsheviks. That was as far as they would go.

Wilson tried diplomacy instead. He proposed a peace conference in early 1919 between the Reds and the Whites. The Bolsheviks were at least prepared to send a delegation to talks, fearful that with the war against Germany won, the Allies would combine forces with the Whites to destroy the Soviet regime. Privately among comrades Lenin said he would be prepared to make a compromise deal with the Whites. But Kolchak refused. The Whites wouldn't discuss any settlement that involved granting any measure of independence to the nationalities.

Their position exasperated Wilson, at a time during the Paris Peace Conference when he was proposing to give self-determination to a number of new countries from the ashes of the Austrian and Ottoman empires. The Americans and the British ditched the Whites, who in truth had lost any chance of winning the war even before. By mid-summer 1919 they were defeated, although isolated groups struggled on for another eighteen months or so. Despite no longer fearing outside attack, the Bolsheviks maintained a 'cordon sanitaire' around Russia and an economic blockade; the regime would not be recognized internationally until the 1930s. For all their victory over the Whites, the Reds still faced opponents internally, but they could be charmed, deceived, intimidated or, finally, terrorized into submission.

Viktor Deni's poster *The Butchers are Torturing Ukraine – Death to the Butchers!* condemns atrocities committed by the Whites. Ukraine was one of the main theatres of the Civil War.

Red victims of the Whites, Siberia, c.1918. Around 450,000 died in the fighting or from disease during Russia's Civil War, but deaths brought about as a result of the war would run into millions.

STATE OF
13 TERROR

13

STATE OF TERROR

AFTER YEARS OF WORLD WAR AND CIVIL WAR, ECONOMIC CHAOS, inflation, starvation for millions and revolution, violence in Russia in the early Soviet years was routine and casual. The streets in Petrograd, Moscow and most Russian cities were not safe. In the rural areas – most of the Russian empire – the abolition of the private estates was accompanied by enormous bloodshed, and the socialization of the land and the 'battle for grain' would bring even more. The Bolsheviks used violence ruthlessly and turned it into an ideology. 'We were always for revolutionary war. The bayonet is an essential necessity for introducing Communism,' remarked one of the cleverest of the early Bolsheviks, Karl Radek (who was on the 'sealed train' with Lenin in 1917, but died a violent death in a labour camp under Stalin). The use of political violence in Russia was endemic; the Bolsheviks did not introduce it, but they did industrialize it.

Life was cheap – a fact that applied to royalty and to the new magnates of Communism. Five weeks after the former Tsar Nicholas and his closest family were murdered, on the night of 16 July 1918 in a dank Yekaterinburg basement, an assassination attempt nearly succeeded in killing Lenin at a Moscow factory.

The basement of the Ipatiev House in Yekaterinburg, where
the Tsar and all his family were murdered in July 1918.

There has never been a paper trail proving that Lenin gave the
order for the murder of the Romanovs – the Bolsheviks claimed that
it was 'local' Party officials in the Urals who sanctioned and executed
the grisly deed and for many years denied that the Tsar's wife, son
and daughters had been killed with him. But without a shadow of
doubt Lenin and his number two at the time, Sverdlov, authorized
the murders. A political decision of that magnitude would never have
been made without their say so. And, as usual, it was Trotsky who gave
the simplest and most persuasive explanation to justify it.

It was thought that we shouldn't leave the Whites a live banner
to rally around [...] The decision was not only expedient but
necessary. It showed everyone that we would continue to fight,

stopping at nothing. It was needed not only to frighten, horrify and instil a sense of hopelessness in the enemy but to shake up our own ranks, to show there was retreating, that ahead lay either total victory or total doom.

When Lenin was shot at the end of August 1918, there was no proof that it was a plot by the Left Socialist Revolutionaries, as has always seemed possible, or was – more likely – the handiwork of one lone gunwoman, Fanny Kaplan, who was summarily executed two days later. One bullet went through Lenin's body and missed a main artery to his heart by a couple of centimetres. Another was lodged in his neck, where it was left by doctors for some time. In the short term he recovered fairly quickly from his injuries, but his bouts of ill health that led to the series of strokes that killed him at the start of 1924 dated from the assassination attempt. In his last two years he was rendered physically and mentally incapable, wheelchair-bound and for long periods unable to speak or use his right arm.

———★———

Yakov Yurovsky, chief jailer of the Romanovs during their months of captivity in Yekaterinburg. Yurovsky also led the firing squad that killed the Russian royal family.

TERROR AS AN ORGANIZED political weapon began in the immediate aftermath of the attempt on the leader's life in August 1918. The Bolsheviks had 'disappeared' opponents after October 1917, but in a haphazard and unpredictable way – and the number of victims was relatively small, in the low hundreds in the first nine months. From now on, however, terror would be carried out on a large scale. By the time of Fanny Kaplan's execution the Bolsheviks had begun an orgy of revenge violence throughout major cities and towns.

The Cheka was unleashed. In Petrograd two days after Lenin was shot 500 prisoners were immediately executed. The following week there were 300 more. Former Tsarist officials and Socialist Revolutionaries were shot in public. In Nizhny Novgorod, forty-one people were executed in the afternoon after Lenin was shot. Their names were published and the local Cheka warned that 'to every murder of a Communist or an attempt at such a murder we shall reply by shooting bourgeois hostages'. The same was happening throughout the country. Altogether 6,185 death sentences were issued in the two months after Lenin was shot, but it is certain that many more people were killed.

From now on there were practically no restraints on the Cheka. The message was that they could do more or less what they wished.

The terror became so casual that some people were slaughtered by ghastly mistake. At a Sovnarkom meeting in October 1919 commissars were discussing investment in railways. Halfway through, Lenin wrote a note to Dzerzhinsky asking, 'How many dangerous counterrevolutionaries do we have in prison?' The Cheka boss scribbled a reply, 'Around 1,500,' and returned the note to Lenin who read it, placed an X by the answer and returned it to Dzerzhinsky. That night hundreds of prisoners in Moscow were executed. As his secretary, Lydia Fotieva, explained later, Lenin had not ordered them to be killed. Sometimes he placed a cross by documents he had seen merely to show that he had read the information and taken note of it.

So routine had the imposition of revolutionary justice become that this appalling error barely caused a stir of any kind. It was all part of the 'war Communism' that for decades to come would exist in the soon to be renamed Union of Soviet Socialist Republics along with rationing, the requisition of land, the continuing war against the *kulaks*, the routine use of slave labour to build infrastructure projects and the construction of the camps of the Gulag system.

To begin with Red Terror was designed to cow the bourgeoisie and obvious opponents into submission, but as the nineteenth-century Russian radical Alexander Herzen predicted, 'Revolution devours its children mercilessly'. Soon it was loyal Party members who were purged – a process that began, typically enough, with a secret protocol that was never discussed among most of the leadership. The Bolsheviks had always emphasized order and Party obedience above all other principles, from the time of *What is to be Done?* in 1902 onwards. The basis of the Party structure, as created by Lenin, was built on the concept of 'democratic centralism' (no irony intended with the first word). Each rung of the Party, from the smallest factory cell to the Central Committee, obeys the decisions of the rung above – a rule enforced rigidly, literally to the point of death. In 1920 Lenin personally wrote a resolution 'On Party Unity', kept secret for many years. It banned all independent factions and groupings that were not recognized by the highest body in the Kremlin, the Politburo, on pain of immediate expulsion from the Party, with no appeal. 'No faction of any sort will be tolerated,' it said. This was to have the gravest consequences for millions of loyal Communists over the coming decades. It was the principal weapon that Stalin would use against 'deviationists' – or anyone he perceived to be an opponent, but it was introduced by Lenin.*

---

* For those who think of this as antediluvian, a museum piece of arcane ideology, a similar clause – almost exactly word for word – exists still in the rule book of the Chinese Communist Party.

—★—

STARVATION WAS NOT uncommon in Russia. There had been famines in 1906 and again in the year before the First World War. But the Great Volga famine in 1921 was by far the worst since the horror a young Vladimir Ulyanov had witnessed in his home region of rural Russia in 1891–2. A crop failure in 1920, followed by a heavy frost and a swelteringly hot summer, were serious natural disasters. However, the catastrophe the following year was caused more by man than by nature.

The main reason was the Soviet regime's continued policy of grain requisitioning. Peasants had been used to maintaining stocks to see themselves through times of bad harvests. Now they grew just enough for subsistence, to feed their livestock and to keep enough seed to sow the next harvest. What was the point of producing more if the Bolsheviks took it all? By 1920 the sown area of the Volga region had declined by 25 per cent in three years. When a poor harvest came there were no reserves of stock.

The Volga region was the worst hit but there was mass starvation in Ukraine, the Urals and Kazakhstan. In Samara province it was estimated that 2 million people were dying of hunger, more than two-thirds of the population – around 700,000 died over the next two years. A quarter of the peasantry in Russia were starving, but for more than a year the government denied there was any significant problem. The words 'famine' and 'starvation' were banned in the press. It was left to a few individuals to begin relief efforts. Gorky appealed for international help and Herbert Hoover, who a few years later would become President of the United States, offered aid from the American Relief Administration, which was feeding millions of people in Western Europe.

Starving peasants in the Volga region, c.1921–2. Drought, together with the agricultural disruption caused by the Revolution and Civil War, brought about a catastrophic famine in Russia in 1921.

Initially the Bolsheviks rejected aid of any kind but relented when they saw that refusing help would look bad internationally. Nevertheless relief workers were spied on by the Cheka.

The famine was accompanied by peasants' revolts throughout the country. The Red Army was used to suppress dozens of rebellions in 1920–1 and were authorized to use poison gas in some areas against bands of peasants armed with a few hundred rifles.

—★—

THE ONE INSTITUTION that continued to resist was the Orthodox Church. Christianity and the Bolsheviks' brand of Communism were bound to collide, eventually. For the first three years the regime was careful and relied on propaganda. After the Whites were defeated and the rebel peasants pacified, the Bolsheviks seized this moment to strike at the Church – on an issue which they hoped would win them popular support.

Under the *ancien régime*, the Church had a unique position of immense temporal as well as spiritual power. The Orthodox faith alone had the right to proselytize; it received generous state subsidies which paid most of the salaries of 45,000 parish priests and financed thousands of monasteries. It was one of the biggest landowners in Russia. Church attendance had been falling sharply for a decade before the February Revolution, but Russia was still a predominantly Orthodox country. Orthodoxy and Tsardom were united in an inseparable link – the Church was effectively a department of State, with its own minister. Historically its politics were ultra-reactionary.

One of the Bolsheviks' first decrees separated Church and State, recognized civil marriages, banned the teaching of religion in state schools and took away all the Church's state funding – fairly moderate steps in a revolution led by fanatical atheists. A new Patriarch, the Metropolitan of Moscow, Tikhon, chose to clash with the Bolsheviks from the start. He deplored 'these monsters of the human race [...] the open and concealed enemies [...] of Christ who have begun to persecute the Church and are striving to destroy Christ's cause'.

There were a few isolated attacks on some priests, but they were not official policy at this stage. Lenin was quite specific in his instructions to the Cheka, which were to leave the Church alone – for now. 'Be very careful in handling the Church. Do nothing hasty. There will come a time for this battle, but wait,' he wrote to Dzerzhinsky early in 1918. When the Communist leaders were 'anathematized' by Tikhon, they simply ignored the prelate.

In the summer of 1919 the government began to seize Church land and property, as it had already done from the big landowners. The regime introduced tougher rules against teaching religion in public places such as parks. Tikhon complained that 'this aims to make impossible the very existence of churches, church institutions and the clergy'. He was put under house arrest for a few months and around 100 priests were arrested.

Then the famine came and Lenin saw the opportunity for attack. Tikhon offered to give the State a substantial amount of money and 'church treasure – except for holy consecrated vessels' for famine relief. In summer 1921 Lenin launched a propaganda campaign throughout the press saying the Church was 'hoarding its treasures' and demanding that it hand over more of its 'hidden wealth [...] so we can turn gold into bread'. If it refused, the property would be confiscated. When Tikhon replied that it would be sacrilege to use consecrated items for secular purposes, Lenin sent Cheka officers to loot the churches.

Lenin deliberately used the famine as an excuse to launch an assault on the clergy: 'It is precisely now, when in the starving regions people are eating human flesh, and thousands of corpses are littering the roads [...] that we must carry out the confiscation of church valuables, with the most merciless energy and crush any resistance,' Lenin wrote in a letter to a Party magnate kept secret until the collapse of the Soviet Union in 1991.

It is now, and only now, that the peasant mass will be for us, or at any rate will not be in a condition to support the clergy [...] We will be unable to do so later because no other moment except that of desperate hunger will give us support among the masses. The confiscations must be conducted with merciless determination [...] the greater the number of clergy and reactionary bourgeoisie we succeed in executing for this reason [i.e., resisting church looting] the better. We must teach these people a lesson so they will not dare even to think of resistance for decades.

This was the violent beginning of the suppression of religion, which over the next fifteen years saw more than 97 per cent of the Soviet Union's churches, synagogues and mosques closed down. Within two years of Lenin's edict more than thirty bishops and 1,200 priests had been killed and thousands more jailed.

—★—

FOR MANY OLDER idealistic socialists in Russia and abroad, the event that did most to shatter hopes and dreams for freedom under the Revolution was the brutal suppression of the sailors at the naval base of Kronstadt. They had played a major role in Bolshevik propaganda as the vanguard of the vanguard which had won power for the Bolsheviks. Sailors from Kronstadt formed the crew of the cruiser *Aurora*, which had shelled the Winter Palace. Scores of them had become Red Guards during the Civil War. They were considered the radical hard men of the Bolshevik Party, totally loyal to the cause and to the leadership. Trotsky called them 'the pride and joy of the Revolution'. Lenin said that when the Revolution was in danger 'we can't fail because we have the sailors with us'.

The Kronstadt sailors began to show dissent at the end of 1920. Their complaints began with economic demands for higher rations and action on relieving food shortages for their families in the villages and in working-class areas of the cities. This was just about acceptable criticism. It was when they began to make political demands that they clashed with the regime.

On 28 February 1921 a mass meeting of sailors on two battleships, the *Petropavlovsk* and the *Sevastopol*, drew up a resolution demanding free elections to a new parliament; free trade unions independent of the Communist Party, a free press, the abolition of the Cheka – and a range of other broadly democratic reforms. The next day there was a demonstration of 16,000 sailors in the centre of the Kronstadt barracks town, where the demands were read out again by the young man who became the sailors' leader, a twenty-one-year-old petty officer on the *Sevastopol*, Stepan Petrichenko.

A small group of naval ratings seized the printing plant, peacefully, and started publishing a newspaper, the Kronstadt *Izvestia*. At no stage did they threaten violence or move in any way against Petrograd, which they could have shelled from their gun batteries, or blockaded if they had chosen to. They had planned no uprising; theirs was a spontaneous expression of disappointment and anger. But immediately the magnates in the Kremlin saw them as a threat. Trotsky declared that if the sailors didn't climb down 'they will be shot like partridges'.

On 4 March, 20,000 Red Army troops arrived in Kronstadt, and Trotsky now issued an ultimatum demanding the rebellious ships submit immediately to the authority of the Soviet Republic.

There was no reply. On 7 March the Bolsheviks – prominent among whose commanders was a young Mikhail Tukhachevsky* – launched their attack: the shore batteries opened fire and soldiers attacked the naval base in a snowstorm. Petrichenko made one last emotional appeal to the Party bosses:

Barely three years ago, you – Lenin, Trotsky, Zinoviev and all of you

---

* Tukhachevsky, who later achieved the rank of Marshal of the Soviet Union, would become a high-profile victim of Stalin's purges of the 1930s.

The Soviets' most prominent educational propaganda poster,
Alexei Radakov's superb *The Illiterate Man is the Blind Man* (1921).

– were denounced as traitors and German spies. We, the workers and sailors, had to come to your rescue and saved your skins [...] It is we who placed you in power [...] Have you forgotten? Now you threaten us with the sword. You are playing with fire. You are repeating the blunders and crimes of Kerensky. Beware that a similar fate doesn't overtake you.

The rebels managed to repulse the Bolshevik attacks for more than a week – but in the end it was a massacre. Nearly all the sailors who survived the final assault on 17 March were summarily executed. Petrichenko and around a hundred others managed to escape to Finland. But thousands died on the frozen lake around Kronstadt. When it was over the Finnish government demanded that the Soviets remove the bodies from the ice. Otherwise the dead would have been swept to Finland's shores when the thaw came. After the savagery of the treatment meted out to their own, the cream of Bolshevik revolutionaries, few people anywhere would be under any illusions that the Bolsheviks would brook any serious opposition.

EPILOGUE

FOR FANATICAL IDEOLOGUES WHO DEDICATED THEIR LIVES TO one set of socialist goals, the Bolsheviks possessed remarkably pragmatic abilities to bend with the wind. After the Kronstadt rebellion and the peasants' revolts the new Soviet regime changed policy 180 degrees and abandoned most of the economic policies introduced since the October Revolution. Factories had stopped producing; money was worthless, there was mass starvation, Russia was exporting nothing. 'War Communism' had not worked and big changes were needed – revolutionary changes.

The government ditched the major economic experiments of the previous three years: the ban on private manufacturing, wholesale nationalization, the seizure of peasant 'surpluses', the replacement of private trade with barter and the partial attempt to abolish money. Lenin now planned a 'tactical retreat' that would become known as the New Economic Policy (NEP). The requisitioning of grain was to be replaced by a 'tax in kind' – and soon by a straightforward money tax. Peasants would be allowed to dispose of any surpluses as they wanted to, implying a return to the private trade of farm produce on the open market. The 'commanding heights' of the economy would remain in state hands – banking, foreign trade, large-scale industry. But the

Lenin defined Communism in his last years as 'Soviets – and electrification'. This, says artist Alexander Samokhvalov's 1923 poster, is 'the Foundation of the new world'.

remaining small enterprises could be leased to the state and run as cooperatives. People were allowed to employ labour once again, which had been banned since 1918. Money made a return and wages were paid in cash, not in kind as had been the custom in many enterprises. Public services and utilities would no longer be free – even investment by 'foreign capitalists' was to be encouraged. The concessions were designed to keep the people from open rebellion. That was the main point of the NEP. 'We are making economic concessions now, in order to avoid making political ones,' admitted Nikolai Bukharin, one of the brains behind the new policy. The Chinese Communists would do something similar under Deng Xiaoping seventy years later: freeing the economy but ensuring the power of the Party remained intact.

At first there was uproar within the Soviet Communist Party. To the idealist true believers – and there were still some left – the NEP seemed like a return to capitalism, an acknowledgement that all their efforts for the last three years had been in vain. To the careerists – of which there were many more – it was a massive risk which they believed would not work and which would reduce their direct authority over people's lives. For the Bolsheviks it was simply about staying in power. They were prepared to give some economic handouts for political survival. It was acknowledged that this was a retreat – 'but the whole army has to make this retreat, united', a Central Committee resolution agreed in the summer 1921.

Lenin admitted that introducing this element of 'state capitalism' – his words – was political rather than economic. 'I appeal to [the Party] that if they don't want the Russian masses to do to them what they did to the Tsar's people, they must throw overboard impracticable daydreams and they must be prepared to face economic laws.'

The NEP stimulated the economy quickly – but it distorted the socialist experiment. In the cities, a new kind of 'Soviet entrepreneur' emerged – extremely rich and brash and showy, but loyal to the Communist Party, nicknamed NEPmen. On the land farmers were producing again and – for now – less fearful that their stock would be seized by the government.

In Moscow everything was available again – for a price. 'Shops and stores sprang up overnight, mysteriously stocked with delicacies Russians had not seen for years,' Emma Goldman, an exile who after the Revolution returned to Russia after twenty years in America, recalled.

> Large quantities of butter, cheese and meat were displayed for sale; pastry, rare fruit and sweets of every variety were to be purchased. Men, women and children with pinched faces and hungry eyes stood about gazing into the windows and discussing the great miracle: what was but yesterday considered a heinous offence was now flaunted before them in an open and legal manner.

When Lenin was asked how long the 'tactical retreat' would last he said, 'For a while, I think [...] not less than ten years.' From now the Bolsheviks talked about modernization and industrialization as quickly as possible, and if that meant elements of capitalism, so be it. Lenin's new definition of Communism would be 'Soviet power, plus electrification'.

And he would slam bureaucracy, which had grown exponentially in a short time – as had the special privileges of the Party apparatchiks, a scar on Communism which would disfigure almost all the societies that attempted socialist revolutions. In the Soviet system – copied elsewhere – each government job from low to mid-level upwards would have a Party shadow, so the number of officials naturally doubled. In the USSR this remained more or less intact until the 1980s. Lenin had seen the problem in 1921: 'We should all be hanged for creating all this unnecessary red tape,' he told one of his chief lieutenants. 'Everything around us is drowned in a filthy swamp of bureaucracy. Over-administration – madness. All these decrees: lunacy. Search for the right people, ensure that the work is properly done – that's all that's necessary.'

He saw that this hydra head of bureaucracy was run by people who on the whole were not up to the job. 'All the evils and hardships we are suffering from [...] are due to the fact that the Communist Party consists of 10 per cent of convinced idealists, ready to die for the cause, but incapable of living for it, and 90 per cent of unscrupulous time-servers who have simply joined the Party to get jobs.' Many of the Leftist critics of the Soviet state for the following decades said pretty much the same thing.

—★—

For many Communists, the Bolsheviks' retreat and abandonment of 'first principles' with the New Economic Policy was the point at which the grand experiment of building their brave new world went wrong. That was when 'cynicism began to eat into the soul of communism', and bureaucratic opportunism took over, as Adolph Joffe, one of the cleverest of the early Bolshevik commissars, put it. For other true believers, cynicism – and opportunism – had done their damage even earlier: from day one of the Bolshevik takeover, when the men and women who made the Revolution accepted that they would make their new world at the point of a gun. What went wrong – and what was to be done about it – has been the subject of vigorous debate on the Left for the best part of a century.

Lenin survived for just two and a half years after he launched the NEP, but for most of that time a series of strokes – like his father, he suffered from lifelong hypertension – had rendered him physically and mentally incapable. He had occasional bouts of lucidity and managed to do some work, but his health was irreparably broken, and he died on 21 January 1924 after lapsing into a coma. Two of the greatest mistakes made by the founder of Russia's Revolution, which were interconnected, resulted in continuing critical problems for decades. Lenin left no system in place for a succession. Having created Stalin – whose character he knew well – and promoted him relentlessly to the top of the Soviet leadership, at the very end of his life Lenin tried, in a secret Testament dictated in December 1922–January 1923, to have Stalin removed from the position of General Secretary of the Russian Communist Party. What would have happened had Lenin succeeded in his attempt constitutes an intriguing counterfactual and a subject for debate. But it was, of course, far too late. By then Stalin had already accrued too much power from the jobs to which Lenin had promoted him. Lenin committed many crimes, but by far the greatest was to have left a man like Stalin in pole position to take over from him.

From the moment the Bolsheviks seized power – illegitimately – they knew it could slip away as swiftly as they had grabbed it. That mindset explains a very great deal of the seventy-four-year history of the Soviet state: its paranoia, ultra-secretiveness, tight hold of centralized power, its casual violence. From the first day of their coup, the principal concern of the early Bolsheviks was to keep the power they had taken – an obsession Lenin and his close comrades passed down to their successors. On the far Left the orthodox argument has been that Lenin and the early Bolsheviks were the idealists and Joseph Stalin (a bureaucratic 'grey blur' in the opinion of the Menshevik Nikolai Sukhanov) the deranged tyrant who stole the state and destroyed the ideals of Communism: the purges, the corruption, the incompetence, the imperial conquests that created an Iron Curtain in Europe and a

Cold War, were the results of Stalinism. I have endeavoured to show here that this is an illusion. It was Lenin and the first Bolsheviks who based their entire political philosophy on the basis that the ends – socialism as Marx and Lenin defined it – justified any means, however bloody. Lenin created the Cheka, the Party's 'sword and shield', which morphed into the KGB and everything those three letters represented. Lenin devised the Gulag. Lenin wrote the clause in the penal code that made 'deviation' and 'factionalism' crimes punishable by death. Stalin perfected the police state and masterminded purges on an industrial scale, but Lenin established all the organs of repression. The seeds of most of the things that went wrong in the Russian Revolution – and why it failed on such an epic scale to perfect humanity – were sown at its very start.

ACKNOWLEDGEMENTS

I AM INDEBTED TO THREE SUPERB BOOKS WHICH HAVE INSPIRED me to write about the Russian Revolution and as a provider of ideas about this subject. The first is Orlando Figes's brilliant and compelling *A People's Tragedy*, the best modern history of the subject. Then Robert Service's magisterial *A History of Twentieth Century Russia*. Third is Simon Sebag Montefiore's *Young Stalin*, which describes in telling detail the horror of revolution, but also the thrill among those involved in one. My enormous thanks to all three.

BIBLIOGRAPHY

Balabanova, Anjelica, *Impressions of Lenin* (Michigan University Press, Ann Arbor, 1964).

Carr, E. H., *The Bolshevik Revolution, 1917–1923* (Penguin, London, 1950).

Conquest, Robert, *The Great Terror* (Penguin, London, 1973).

Figes, Orlando, *A People's Tragedy: The Russian Revolution 1891–1924* (Jonathan Cape, London, 1996).

Figner, Vera, *Memoirs of a Revolutionist* (University of Illinois Press, Champaign, Illinois, 1991).

Hastings, Max, *Catastrophe: Europe Goes to War 1914* (William Collins, London, 2013).

Lenin, V. I., *Selected Texts* (includes *What is To Be Done?*) (Penguin Modern Classics, London, 1990).

Lieven, Dominic, *Nicholas II, Tsar of all the Russias* (John Murray, London, 1993).

McMeekin, Sean, *The Russian Revolution* (Basic Books, New York, 2017).

Pipes, Richard, *The Russian Revolution, 1899–1919* (Fontana, London, 1990).

Reed, John, *Ten Days that Shook the World* (Penguin Modern Classics, London, 2010).

Rhys Williams, Albert, *Through the Russian Revolution* (Liveright, New York, 1921).

Sebag Montefiore, Simon, *Young Stalin* (Weidenfeld & Nicolson, London, 2007).

– *The Romanovs, 1613–1918* (Weidenfeld & Nicolson, London, 2016).

Sebestyen, Victor, *Lenin the Dictator* (Weidenfeld & Nicolson, London, 2017).

Service, Robert, *A History of Modern Russia* (Penguin, London, 2003).

– *A History of Twentieth Century Russia* (Macmillan, London, 1996).

– *Trotsky, A Biography* (Macmillan, London, 2009).

Shukman, Harold (ed.), *The Blackwell Encyclopaedia of the Russian Revolution* (Blackwell, Oxford, 1988).

Struve, Peter, *Collected Works* (Michigan University Press, Ann Arbor, 1970).

Sukhanov, Nikolai, *The Russian Revolution: A Personal Record* (Princeton University Press, Princeton, NJ, 1982).

Swain, Geoffrey, *The Russian Civil War* (The History Press, London, 2008).

Trotsky, Leon, *My Life, An Attempt at an Autobiography* (Scribner, New York, 1930).

– *The History of the Russian Revolution* (Scribner, New York, 1930).

Wilson, Edmund, *To the Finland Station* (Fontana, London, 1972).

The Marxist Internet archive https://www.marxists.org contains a superb range of material by Marx, Lenin, Trotsky and various Communist and Soviet thinkers.

INDEX

and the February
Revolution 84
and the First World War
75–8
requisitions 188–90
'former people' 183, 188
Fotieva, Lydia 215
France 24, 25, 70
Francis, David R. 134
Fredericks, Count Vladimir
88, 91
Frentz, Rudolf
October Night 159
FSB 35
Fundamental Laws 35

Gapon, Father Georgy 55–6
Germany 24, 25
and the First World War
68, 70–1, 74, 119, 120–1
Lenin and the Bolsheviks
107–8, 126–7
Lenin's peace deal with
174–5
and the October
Revolution 194
and the Russian Civil War
203, 204, 206
Sparticist Uprising 134
Gippius, Zinaida 75, 81, 96,
105, 147, 166, 188
Goethe, Johann von 165
Goldman, Emma 228
Gorky, Maxim 56, 60, 84,
95, 104, 115, 145, 166,
187, 217
grain requisitioning 217, 225
Guchkov, Alexander 80, 91
Gulag system 216, 231
Gumilyov, Nikolai 75

Herzen, Alexander 36, 216
Hindenberg, Paul von 71
Hitler, Adolf 10, 63, 107
Hoare, Sir Samuel 78
Hoover, Herbert 217

industrial workers 24
and the Bolsheviks 179

Lenin's decree on Workers'
Rights 172
and Lenin's politics 109
and Marxism 39, 46
and the soviets 96–7
inflation 110, 175, 187, 188
ISIS 44

Japan 54, 55
Jews 93
antisemitism 43, 63–4,
104, 201–3
and the Civil War 201–3
Joffe, Adolphe 172, 229
July Days 129–34, 135
Kadets (Constitutional
Democrats) 90, 99, 126,
129, 135, 145, 169
and Constituent Assembly
elections 179, 180
Kamenev, Boris 145, 167–8
Kandinsky, Wassily 75
Kaplan, Fanny 214, 215
Kayurov, Vladimir 92
Kazakhstan 217
Kazan 200
Kerensky, Alexander 26, 90,
103–6, 109, 124–5, 127, 224
and the army 105, 168
background 103–4
and the Bolsheviks 107, 140,
142, 144, 145, 146, 167
character 104–5
and the First World War
119–20
and the Jews 104
and the July Days 129, 131
and the Kornilov Affair
135–7
and the October
Revolution 146, 147,
151, 155, 194
portrait of 106
and socialism 105
speeches 104, 137
and the Whites 201
see also Provisional
Government
KGB 35, 173, 231

Khabalov, General Sergei 88
Kirpichnikov, Timofey 89
Klembovski, General
Vladislav 114
Knox, Colonel Alfred 111–14
Kolchak, Alexander 198, 206
Kornilov, Lavr 135–6
Kronstadt naval base 131,
151, 181
rebellion 221–4, 225
Krupskaya, Nadezhda
(Lenin's wife) 47, 49, 167,
175
Kühlmann, Richard von 127
kulaks 185–6, 188–9, 216

Land and Liberty 36–8
landowners
and the February
Revolution 115–19
Lansing, Robert 204
legal system 182–5
Lenin, Vladimir Ilyich 8,
10, 12, 29, 35, 38, 39–48,
63, 182
and the 1905 Revolution
57, 62
and antisemitism 203
assassination attempt on
212, 214
on bureaucracy in the
Soviet system 228–9
character 165
and the Civil War 196, 200,
203, 206
and Communism 226
Decree on the Press 169
deviationism 46, 216
education 41
exile 43, 64–5
family background 40–1
in Finland 130, 131, 140–3
ill-health and death 229–30
importance of 18
and inflation 187
and the July Days 130–1,
134
and the Kornilov Affair 137
on the *kulaks* and food

PICTURE CREDITS